COMBAT DIARY

Combat Diary

EPISODES FROM THE HISTORY OF THE TWENTY-SECOND REGIMENT, 1866–1905

A. B. FEUER

Foreword by
General William B. Rosson

Afterword by
Colonel James N. Joyner, Jr.

PRAEGER

New York
Westport, Connecticut
London

Library of Congress Cataloging-in-Publication Data
Feuer, A. B., 1925–
    Combat diary : episodes from the history of the Twenty-second Regiment, 1866–1905 / A. B. Feuer ; foreword by General William B. Rosson ; afterword by Colonel James N. Joyner, Jr.
        p.   cm.
    Based on the diary of Jacob F. Kreps.
    Includes index.
    ISBN 0-275-93929-4 (alk. paper)
    1. United States. Army—Military life. 2. United States. Army. Infantry Regiment, Twenty-second. I. Kreps, Jacob F. II. Title.
U766.F48   1991
355.1'0973—dc20   91-11079

British Library Cataloguing in Publication Data is available.

Copyright © 1991 by A. B. Feuer

All rights reserved. No portion of this book may be reproduced, by any process or technique, without the express written consent of the publisher.

Library of Congress Catalog Card Number: 91-11079
ISBN: 0-275-93929-4

First published in 1991

Praeger Publishers, One Madison Avenue, New York, NY 10010
An imprint of Greenwood Publishing Group, Inc.

Printed in the United States of America

The paper used in this book complies with the Permanent Paper Standard issued by the National Information Standards Organization (Z39.48–1984).

10 9 8 7 6 5 4 3 2 1

Dedicated to

the Past, Present, and Future

Members of

the Twenty-second Infantry Regiment

CONTENTS

MAPS	ix
FOREWORD by General William B. Rosson	xi
ACKNOWLEDGMENTS	xv
INTRODUCTION	xvii
Chapter 1 EARLY U.S. ARMY SERVICE IN THE WEST	1
Chapter 2 LIEUTENANT JACOB KREPS ON THE FRONTIER: 1890–1898	13
Chapter 3 THE CUBAN CAMPAIGN: THE SPANISH-AMERICAN WAR	19
Chapter 4 THE BATTLE OF MANILA	53
Chapter 5 REVOLT IN THE PHILIPPINES	75
Chapter 6 THE MALOLOS CAMPAIGN	95

Chapter 7	THE LAGUNA DE BAY AND SAN MIGUEL CAMPAIGNS	109
Chapter 8	THE CAMPAIGN SOUTH OF MANILA	123
Chapter 9	THE MARCH TO LINGAYEN GULF	131
Chapter 10	THE CHASE OF AGUINALDO EAST TO BAYOMBONG	141
Chapter 11	THE CAPTURE OF AGUINALDO	147
Chapter 12	THE MORO REVOLT	155
Chapter 13	THE MINDANAO CAMPAIGN	163
AFTERWORD by Colonel James N. Joyner, Jr.		175
INDEX		177

Photographs *Following page 94*

MAPS

Map	1.1	The Northern Plains, 1868–1890	2
Map	1.2	The Southwest Plains, 1862–1890	11
Map	3.1	Cuba	20
Map	3.2	Santiago and El Caney Campaigns, July 1, 1898	31
Map	4.1	The Philippine Islands	54
Map	4.2	American, Spanish and Insurgent Positions South of Manila, July 30, 1898	60
Map	5.1	Position of Nebraska Volunteer Regiment and Insurgent Blockhouses, February 2, 1899	77
Map	5.2	Insurgent Blockhouses and La Loma Church Guarding the Approaches to Caloocan	80
Map	5.3	Insurgent-Controlled Towns South of the Pasig River	88
Map	6.1	Towns and Rivers on the Route to Malolos	96
Map	7.1	The Laguna de Bay Area	110

Map 7.2	Northern Luzon, Philippines, the Theater of Operations for the Twenty-second Infantry, 1899–1901	114
Map 8.1	The Campaign Area South of Manila	126
Map 12.1	Mindanao	156
Map 12.2	Lake Lanao Region, Mindanao	158

FOREWORD

The reader of this book will discover historical coverage not only of the Twenty-second Infantry Regiment, an old and distinguished unit, but of numerous other United States Army units—infantry, cavalry, artillery, engineer, medical, quartermaster, and signal. Nor is the coverage confined to the army. Valuable material on the United States Navy and the United States Marine Corps has been interwoven into the fabric of the stories presented by the author.

In its structure, the book embraces United States Army campaigns against the Indians on the western frontier from the close of the Civil War to the early 1890s; the Spanish-American War, 1898; the Philippine Insurrection, 1899–1901; and the Moro revolt, 1904–1905. The treatment of these periods enjoys uncommon authenticity and appeal through use by the author of a diary kept by Jacob F. Kreps, an officer who joined the Twenty-second Infantry Regiment in 1883 as a second lieutenant from West Point, and who served continuously with it over a thirty-five-year career that took him to the rank of colonel. Other documentation is used to complement and extend the accounts provided by Kreps, but it is the latter's personal commentary on combat action—action in which he was a participant—that gives *Combat Diary* a distinctive flavor.

Various writings devoted to the developmental and expansionist period of America's history embody considerable in the way of romantic legend. *Combat Diary* follows in that tradition. As such, it will find favor not only with those who seek new coverage of well-documented history, but with those who savor adventure, manly accomplishment, heroism, sacrifice, and victory over both armed opponents and the elements.

While emphasizing the key material supplied by Colonel Kreps and other primary and secondary sources, the author nonetheless has taken pains to insure that the firsthand accounts of those who were serving in lower level leadership positions are augmented by timely information on the "big picture." (Kreps wrote as a lieutenant and as a captain.) This is done with a deft touch that provides the reader with adequate, but never excessive, treatment. Emphasis on combat action is enhanced by the author's provision of supporting maps and diagrams, which serve additionally to assist the reader in identifying and interrelating places and directions cited in the text.

It is in the domain of insight that *Combat Diary* has much to offer those who are not students of military history, and even for the students there are sure to be new discoveries. The reader will be led to an appreciation of the character of the infantry soldier—indeed, of the United States Army. Matters such as the social, economic, and educational background of the men who served in the ranks, the reasons that motivated men to seek service in the regular army, the system of discipline and the provisions for indoctrination and training will present themselves for thought. By the same token, the quality and influence of officer and noncommissioned officer leadership will impress the reader as being vital ingredients.

Portrayed accurately but without overemphasis are important historical facts such as the mobilization fiasco that accompanied our entry into the Spanish-American War; the monumentally inadequate logistic preparations for that war (woolen uniforms for tropical service, spoilage of rations, loss of ammunition due to ill-conceived ship-to-shore delivery); paucity of medical support not only to deal with battlefield wounds in Cuba, but to contend with yellow fever; and the superiority of the smokeless Mauser rifle used by the Spanish over the shorter range, position-revealing American Springfields. Fortunately, the problems produced by these shortcomings translated into lessons that later were to be utilized in improving the effectiveness of all of the armed forces.

The portions of the book devoted to the Philippine Insurrection bring to the fore a wealth of descriptive detail on small unit engagements, including tactics and techniques. They also focus on problems generated by climate and terrain, and highlight the tenacity and innovativeness displayed by American forces operating in a difficult environment. One is impressed by the fighting esprit manifested by regular and volunteer units alike, and by exceptional officer and noncommissioned officer leadership. As in the case of the treatment of the Spanish-American War, the coverage lends itself to acquisition of insight into the character of the soldier—both leaders and followers.

Significantly, the diary and related sources devote a generous measure of emphasis to America's adversary in the Philippines following the Spanish surrender of Manila in August 1898. The result is a fascinating and instructive portrayal of the Philippine political activist and soldier, Emilio Aguinaldo, and his forces. Here again, however, the author has exercised care not to permit the political-diplomatic side of the Aguinaldo story to dilute the focus on combat between American units and the Insurgents.

Of particular importance is the treatment of the decision by Aguinaldo late in 1899, following a succession of defeats north of Manila, to resort to guerrilla warfare. Thereafter, as the diary accounts reveal, the Americans were confronted with the requirement to operate against both conventional and guerrilla forces, and to adapt to dealing with a civilian population within which loyalties were divided. Comparable requirements were to confront American forces in a neighboring area, Vietnam, beginning six decades later.

In what might be regarded as a postscript, the book provides accounts of American forces employed in a law and order role to suppress fractious Moslem Moro tribal groups on the southern Philippine island of Mindanao. One is taken to the heart of numerous combat actions, various of them noteworthy for evidence of fanaticism among the Moros, whose warriors were known to fight on after having sustained one or more bullet wounds and whose knives, the "kris," commanded deserved respect.

Several excellent reports are to be found on use by the Moros of small forts known as "cottas" and on the difficulty experienced by American units in overcoming them. The Moro segment ends with coverage of a raid on the ranch stronghold of Datto Ali, the last of the resistant Moro chieftains. Accomplished by a small contingent of American regulars who operated by stealth and surprise assault, the operation resulted in the death of Ali and the collapse of resistance without American casualties—the very stuff from which romantic legends are forged!

Combat Diary is a readable, informative, satisfying book. Although its opening treatment of the Indian-fighting era clearly is limited, this is a function of the diary treatment it received, not of disregard on the part of the author. As one moves into the Spanish-American War and beyond, one has begun to tap a richly productive vein. The writer of the diary and other contributors may be guilty of hyperbole here and there, but this common tendency is more than offset by the degree to which they have enhanced understanding of the institutions, the times, and the events of which they wrote. The dominant feeling one will have after reading the book is that of pride in and admiration for the American soldier. A. B. Feuer merits our gratitude for having given us the opportunity to experience that feeling.

William B. Rosson
General, U.S. Army (Ret.)

ACKNOWLEDGMENTS

I would like to thank General William B. Rosson (U.S. Army, Retired) for his assistance in preparing this manuscript. General Rosson's proficient knowledge of the infantry and of the history of the Spanish-American War era has added an authoritative perspective to life in the professional army.

I am also indebted to Colonel James Joyner, Jr., Professor of Military Science at the Virginia Military Institute. Colonel Joyner's association with the Twenty-second Infantry helped immeasurably with documentation of the regiment's history.

In addition, I would like to express my appreciation to the United States Military Academy Archives for the information that they provided on Colonel Kreps.

Photographs are courtesy of the National Archives, U.S. Army Military History Institute, Montana Historical Society, and the Arizona Historical Society.

INTRODUCTION

On the brittle pages of a ledger-sized notebook, Jacob Kreps eloquently related with pen and pencil his personal experiences as an officer with the Twenty-second Infantry Regiment of the United States Army.

Kreps served with this celebrated unit throughout the exciting expansionistic period of American history—on the western frontier, and during the Spanish-American War and Philippine Insurrection.

Among the memorabilia of Jacob Kreps, and also quoted in this manuscript, is an extremely rare regimental history of the Twenty-second Infantry. The fragile, digest-sized book was privately printed in the Philippines in 1905—and comprises the experiences of members of the regiment as edited by Major O. M. Smith and Captains Robert L. Hamilton and William H. Wassell. Jacob Kreps contributed several of his own exploits to the unique document. This particular copy, signed by Captain Hamilton, was autographed by Jacob Kreps to his wife, Helen Amelia, on February 20, 1906—a belated Valentine gift.

In addition to the handwritten diary and regimental history, four interesting scrapbooks (presumably put together by Helen Kreps) contain newspaper articles and other accounts of the Spanish-American War and Insurrection. These intriguing items were meticulously pasted to thick pages, which are now time-yellowed, and follow the Twenty-second Infantry and other regiments through Cuba and the Philippine Islands.

The tactics and strategies as narrated by the soldiers of the Twenty-second—who fought more than one hundred battles—are from an infantryman's point of view. Jacob Kreps had his own personal opinions concerning the plans of his superiors, but he obeyed orders—even though he knew that they would cost lives.

However, one thing is certain, Jacob Kreps was a soldier's soldier. Throughout his more than thirty-year career in the army, the welfare of his men—from private on up—was his primary concern. He was indeed a credit to his country and the United States Army.

For a better understanding of what occurred in the Philippines prior to the arrival of the Twenty-second Infantry, a chapter has been devoted to the first three expeditions to the islands and the Battle of Manila.

Also quoted in this story are several battlefield action reports as recorded by General Marcus Wright in *Leslie's Official History of the Spanish-American War*, printed by the War Record Office in 1899. Additional Philippine data was researched from Irving Faust's *Campaigning in the Philippines*, published in 1905.

COMBAT DIARY

Chapter One

EARLY U.S. ARMY SERVICE IN THE WEST

During the War of 1812, the Twenty-second Infantry Regiment participated in eight battles. Its final engagement of the conflict was the siege and assault on Fort Erie in August and September 1814.

From 1815 until 1861, the regiment was a part of the Second Infantry. With the beginning of the Civil War, individual companies were brought together and organized as the First and Second Battalions of the Thirteenth Infantry Regiment.

Throughout the war, the First Battalion fought numerous engagements under the command of William T. Sherman and Philip H. Sheridan. There are few records of the Second Battalion's activities.

In April 1866, the Twenty-second Infantry (it was still designated as the Thirteenth Infantry until September of that year) was divided between forts in the Dakota Territory.

Company C was sent to Fort Buford—which at that time was nothing more than a tent camp with seventy enlisted men and two officers. Captain W. G. Rankin's orders were to "build a post." The army was unconcerned that the only tools the men had to work with were handaxes, but that was the least of Rankin's troubles—hostile Indians attacked the campsite practically every day.

Squads of soldiers, cutting and rafting logs from the mouth of the Yellowstone River, were often pounced upon and driven back to camp. The ensuing battles would last from two to six hours.

Captain Robert Lee Hamilton wrote: "These were trying times for

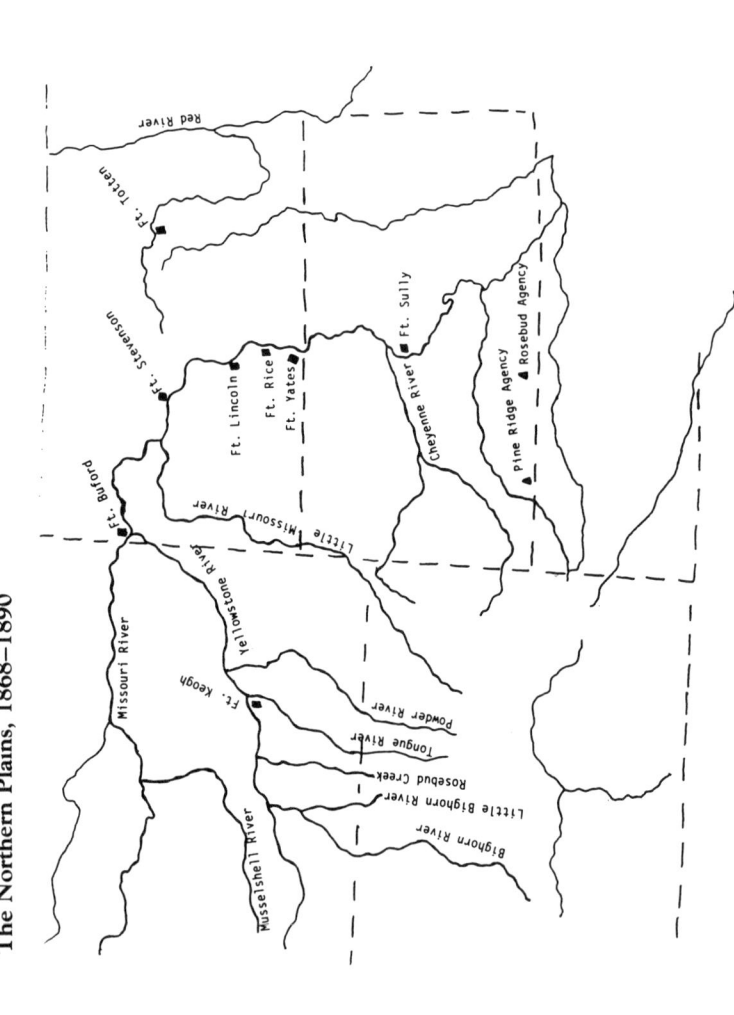

Map 1.1
The Northern Plains, 1868–1890

the small detachment of soldiers at Fort Buford. The Sioux had been heavily reinforced, and boldly boasted that they intended to annihilate the soldiers.

"Throughout the harsh winter, the post was continually besieged. The troops were virtually cut off from water [Missouri River] and were forced to sink wells near their quarters.

"Until spring, only two mails managed to leave the fort, and rumors spread east that the garrison had been massacred. Captain Rankin's wife spent the winter in camp with her husband—bravely enduring the hardship and danger."

By the summer of 1867, two more posts were under construction—Fort Stevenson and Fort Totten. Working squads carried their guns with them, and, when surprised by Indians, they would form a battle line and fight off the warriors.

Large building logs were scarce—at times many miles from the fort site. Armed escorts were sent with the wagons that carried the logging parties. However, they were often attacked by the Sioux—both sides suffering heavy casualties.

Captain Hamilton stated: "The troops lived in tents until late in the winter of 1867. The snow was waist deep before they were able to move into warm quarters.

"It was none too soon at Stevenson and Totten, as a furious snowstorm lashed the forts for several days with savage winds, followed by bitter cold. Officers and men remained inside their quarters until the storm abated. At Stevenson, fuel ran out and the soldiers burned furniture to keep from freezing.

"A wagon train, loaded with lumber and canned goods, en route from Fort Abercrombie to Totten, was forced to halt at the Cheyenne River. In order to keep from freezing and starving, the men burned the lumber and ate most of the canned food."

Official correspondence and mail arrived at the forts every two weeks during the winter—once a month at more distant posts. The mail was carried by dog sled, and half-breeds were employed as drivers.

Captain Hamilton narrated: "Communication between Stevenson and Buford—and between Totten and Stevenson was difficult. This section of territory was infested with hostile Indians—who would attack the mail parties and wipe them out to the man.

"In the Spring of 1868, a squad of soldiers left Totten with dispatches for Stevenson. About midway between the two posts, the troops were ambushed by a large number of Sioux. A rescue party later found the soldiers' bodies—stripped of clothing and mutilated."

In the meantime, the men of the Twenty-second Regiment were busy constructing Forts Sully and Rice. Detachments were also sent to occupy Indian agencies, where they were often attacked.

During the summer of 1868, a group of Sioux raided a cattle herd at Fort Buford. Three officers were wounded and several soldiers killed. The cattle were stampeded and driven off.

During this period, on the frontier, there was not one mile of railway in the Dakotas and Montana—and not more than three stage lines operated in the two territories. Captain Hamilton wrote how difficult it was to travel from one post to another without a military escort: "In 1870, three officers of the Twenty-second Infantry were ordered from Fort Sully to Fort Totten—a distance, as the crow flies, of 250 miles. They were required to travel by way of Sioux City, Chicago, and St. Paul—more than 1,600 miles to reach their destination."

In the fall of 1871, a surveying party headed for the Yellowstone River was organized at Fort Rice. The purpose was to plot the path of the Northern Pacific Railroad. Units of the Seventeenth, Twentieth, and Twenty-second Infantries accompanied the group. The troops were under the command of Colonel Whistler. Besides six companies of soldiers, the expedition consisted of 104 wagons, twenty-six Indian scouts, and two Gatling guns.

The survey detail departed Fort Rice on September 9, and reached the Yellowstone, at the mouth of the Glendive Creek, on October 2. They immediately headed back to Fort Rice—covering the 300 miles (on foot) in only fourteen days—four of which were spent resting at campsites.

The following year, another expedition to the Yellowstone was mobilized under the command of Major General David S. Stanley. The troops included companies of the Eighth, Seventeenth, and Twenty-second Infantries—plus a platoon of Indian scouts. Captain Hamilton stated: "The expedition marched from Fort Rice on July 26, arriving at the mouth of the Powder River on August 18. During the afternoon, General Stanley, accompanied by several officers, parleyed with a group of Indians headed by Gaul. The Indians stood on the opposite side of the river. Suddenly, one of Gaul's braves opened fire. Our troops rallied to the spot, and the Indians beat a retreat. We then returned back to Rice, skirmishing with hostiles twice on the return march."

During May 1873, a third trip to the Yellowstone was planned with General Stanley again serving as commanding officer. The expedition consisted of the Seventh Cavalry—units of the Sixth, Eighth, Ninth, Seventeenth, and Twenty-second Infantries—along with a detachment of scouts.

Captain Hamilton described the journey: "On June 20, we departed Fort Rice with a large wagon train—arriving July 31 at the crossing of the Yellowstone about fifteen miles above Glendive. We advanced up the left bank of the river as far as Pompey's Pillar—but not without opposition from the Indians. They evidently had concluded that our surveying had gone far enough.

"On August 4, just opposite where Fort Keogh now stands, a band of Indians ambushed our advance guard, killing three men. The Seventh Cavalry dashed to the attack—driving the enemy off with heavy losses.

"A few days later, the cavalry encountered a large force of Indians near the mouth of the Bighorn River. A desperate fight ensued with loss of life on both sides. However, upon approach of the infantry, the hostiles dispersed.

"That evening, the Twenty-second Regiment occupied the advance posts. Shots were exchanged with the Indians throughout the night as they tried to approach the camp—probably to stampede our horses and cattle herd.

"The following day, our artillery shelled the timber along the banks of the Yellowstone—in order to dislodge a band of Indians who were evidently preparing to impede the next day's journey.

"The expedition continued on to the Musselshell River—thence to the Great Porcupine—following the river until we again reached the Yellowstone.

"This was entirely new and unexplored country—and it was very difficult to transport a large military force and wagon train across unmapped territory. Water was the most pressing problem—it was either alkaline, or none at all. Our weary command finally arrived at Fort Lincoln on September 22."

In early 1874, the Twenty-second Regiment changed stations with the First Infantry—which had been garrisoned at forts along the Great Lakes. This was a new and happy experience for the suntanned frontier fighters—but it proved to be of short duration.

Disturbances in New Orleans, by an organization known as the "White League," prompted the Army Department to send seven companies of the Twenty-second Regiment to that city in an effort to maintain order. It had been intimated that the duty would be only for about ten days. Instead, the troops were quartered in various parts of the city for eight months.

On the afternoon of June 25, 1876, General George Armstrong Custer and 210 men of the Seventh Cavalry lost their lives at the Little Bighorn. When the news of the tragedy reached the soldiers of the Twenty-second, the troops were devastated—many had personal friends among the men who had lost their lives. "If only we had been there," was a phrase that was repeated over and over again.

A feeling of guilt spread through the regiment, and an immediate request for transfer to the frontier was dispatched to Washington.

A battalion of the Twenty-second Regiment was quickly ordered into the field. It was placed under the command of Lieutenant Colonel Elwell S. Otis and directed to join the forces of General Alfred H. Terry at the mouth of the Rosebud River in Montana.

Lieutenant Colonel Otis and his battalion, composed of eight companies, traveled to the Rosebud by way of the Yellowstone River. They marched aboard the steamship *Carroll*, along with new recruits for the decimated Seventh Cavalry.

On July 29, while the *Carroll* was passing the mouth of the Powder River, a large band of Indians on the right bank of the Yellowstone attacked the steamer. Captain Hamilton narrated: "We responded promptly. The *Carroll* beached on the riverbank and three companies splashed ashore. The fight lasted for some time, engaged in by the troops aboard ship, as well as the men on land. After a few hours, the Indians retreated back into the hills. We burned their camp and confiscated firearms and ammunition."

The battalion arrived at General Terry's camp on the first of August—and a week later began a reconnaissance up the Rosebud River. Hamilton wrote: "The valley of the lower Rosebud is very rough, and the marches were short and difficult. In the forenoon of the 10th, there was great excitement. Heavy dust was seen rising two or three miles to our front, and rapidly approaching horsemen were observed. Rumors passed down the line that hostiles were ahead, and a battle could be expected within a few minutes.

"However, much to the disappointment of many of the men, the unrecognized riders proved to be William F. Cody [Buffalo Bill] and several of his scouts."

For the next few weeks, Otis and his battalion were constantly on the march—following Indian trails along the Rosebud, Tongue, and Powder Rivers. They then crossed to the north side of the Yellowstone and marched to the junction of the Missouri River.

Not one Indian was seen—but the soldiers knew they were out there—watching every move that the army made.

On August 31, 1876, Elwell Otis received instructions to keep his troops in Montana throughout the winter. The battalion camped at the mouth of Glendive Creek and commenced constructing huts for their winter quarters.

A few companies were delegated to escort supply trains to infantry units camped at the mouth of the Tongue River—later to be the site of Fort Keogh.

Captain Hamilton recorded the dangers of traveling from one post to another: "On October 10, three companies of the Twenty-second were accompanying a wagon train from Glendive to the Tongue River station. That night, they camped at Spring Creek. About three o'clock the following morning, the campsite was vigorously attacked by a large group of Indians. The surprise raid was repulsed, but our mules became excited and escaped from the corral. More than forty of the animals fell into hostile hands, and the train was so crippled that it was forced to return to Glendive."

Upon the return of the wagons, Lieutenant Colonel Otis reorganized the supply convoy, and on the 14th, he set out again for the Tongue River—this time with five companies of troops.

Hamilton continued: "At seven o'clock on the morning of the 15th, we were 12 miles above Glendive. Suddenly, without warning, about a thousand Sioux swooped down on us. It was a desperate fight—lasting until seven that evening. The Indians tried every trick to capture the train—including setting fire to the prairie grass through which the troops and wagons had to pass.

"The enemy was finally driven off—suffering heavy casualties. We expected that the Indians would renew their attack in the morning. And, by first light, we could see them—mounted in large numbers on our left flank."

Elwell Otis was not intimidated by his enemy's show of strength. The order was given for the wagon train and troops to move out. The convoy continued its journey under the watchful eyes of hundreds of Sioux warriors stationed motionless on the crest of the hills.

Only a few miles had been traveled, when an Indian runner approached and planted a spear in the ground—about a hundred yards ahead of the lead wagon. A message could be seen tied to the lance. An army scout rushed forward, grabbed the communique, and delivered it to Otis:

Yellowstone, I want to know what you are doing traveling on this road. You scare all the buffalo away. I want to hunt on the place. I want you to turn back from here. If you do not, I will fight you again. I want you to leave what you have got here and turn back from here. I mean all the rations you have got and some powder. Wish you would write as soon as you can. I am your friend, Sitting Bull.

Lieutenant Colonel Otis immediately sent word back to the Indian chief that the soldiers intended to take the wagon train all the way to Tongue River, and "would be pleased to accommodate Sitting Bull at any time with a fight."

Hamilton described what happened next: "The Indians gathered again on the bluffs—as if to begin battle. But, after a few minutes, a Sioux delegation bearing a flag of truce approached our lines. After a parley, the Indians decided that they were tired of fighting and wanted peace."

During the month of December, several companies of the Twenty-second Regiment participated in Colonel Nelson A. Miles' successful campaign against Sitting Bull and Crazy Horse at the Bighorn Mountains.

The troops returned to the Tongue River in January 1877. However, the winter snowstorms and freezing temperatures had taken a heavy toll on the soldiers.

When spring arrived, Colonel Miles put together another expedition consisting of the Second Cavalry, and companies of the Fifth and Twenty-second Infantry Regiments. Also included was a detachment of the Twenty-second's Indian scouts under the command of Lieutenant Edward Casey.

On April 30, the army brigade marched out from camp—its mission, to search out a band of renegade Indians under the leadership of Lame Deer. The outlaw group was rumored to be located near the Rosebud, but a necessary detour on the Tongue River made the journey a 100-mile trip.

After traveling about sixty miles up the Tongue, Colonel Miles halted his troops. The Fifth Infantry was assigned to guard the wagons, while the cavalry, the Twenty-second Infantry, and Casey's scouts made a forced march upstream. They crossed the Rosebud, and traveled two nights and a day with scarcely a halt.

On the early morning of May 7, the soldiers discovered Lame Deer's campsite. Captain Hamilton stated: "We attacked the still sleeping Indians near the mouth of Muddy Creek. Lieutenant Casey and his scouts were the first to sneak in. They surrounded the camp and made off with a herd of 450 ponies.

"Before the Indians realized what was happening, Lieutenant Jerome and his Second Cavalry dashed through the encampment. The Indians opened fire, but the element of surprise was too great and mass confusion resulted.

"As soon as the commotion began to die down, we called upon the Indians to surrender. Lame Deer, and his chief warrior Iron Star, appeared ready to do so—but several of the young braves commenced shooting at our troops. That ended the peace-making. The fight was resumed and the enemy retreated into the hills. Among the Indian dead were Lame Deer and Iron Star.

"The companies of the Twenty-second Infantry took their positions around the area. Sporadic firing between the troops and Indians was kept up the entire night—we had little sleep.

"The next morning, the renegade camp was burned and we headed back toward the Tongue River. With such a large number of captured ponies, every soldier had a horse to ride."

In late May, the Twenty-second Regiment Battalion was consolidated under the command of Colonel Hough, and marched out to the Black Hills, following the trail of Lame Deer's disciples. Lieutenant Casey's scouts led the way—at times coming so close to the enemy that the scouts suffered heavy losses from Indian attacks.

The outlaw camp was soon located in the badlands of the Little Missouri near Sentinel Bluffs, but by the time the army arrived in force, the Indians had abandoned the site. The Twenty-second Regiment then made a forced march to Fort Lincoln.

There was no time for rest—the battalion was immediately ordered to Chicago to suppress railroad riots. After several days, quiet was restored. However a well-deserved tour of garrison duty was still a long way off. New directives were issued sending the weary soldiers to Wilkesbarre, Pennsylvania to keep peace in the mining districts.

During the year 1877, the battalion had marched more than three thousand miles.

In April 1879, the regiment received orders to join the Department of Texas. However, while en route, four companies under the command of Colonel Hough were sent to Fort Gibson to quell an Indian disturbance. The other units of the regiment were assigned to Fort McKavett and Fort Griffin.

Later that year, a conflict with the Ute Indians of Colorado was anticipated. Colonel Hough's troops were dispatched to Ouray, where they prevented the northern Ute tribes from joining the southern Utes and starting a general war.

In January 1880, Hough was ordered back to Fort Gibson. Because of deep snow in the mountains, his men were compelled to march five hundred miles to Santa Fe, New Mexico, and then by rail to Gibson.

The Twenty-second Regiment remained in Texas, serving at various posts, until November 1882, when it was transferred to the Department of Missouri. One company was quartered at Santa Fe, and the others split between the Colorado forts of Garland, Lewis, and Lyon.

In September 1885, units of the regiment alternated guarding passes through the Datil Hills and fighting off hostile Apaches. This hazardous duty continued until April the following year, when the companies returned to their stations at the Colorado forts for several months of quiet garrison activity.

However, there was no rest for Lieutenant Casey and his scouts. They were sent on a survey mission to the Grand Canyon. The detachment returned to Fort Lewis on January 5, 1888—having covered nearly eight hundred miles. Most of the territory had never been mapped.

During the month of May, the regiment changed station to the Department of Dakota. Seven companies were sent to Fort Keogh, while the others were assigned to Totten and Lincoln. The Twenty-second Regiment now began a period of service in the northwest, which was to last seven years.

Map 1.2
The Southwest Plains, 1862–1890

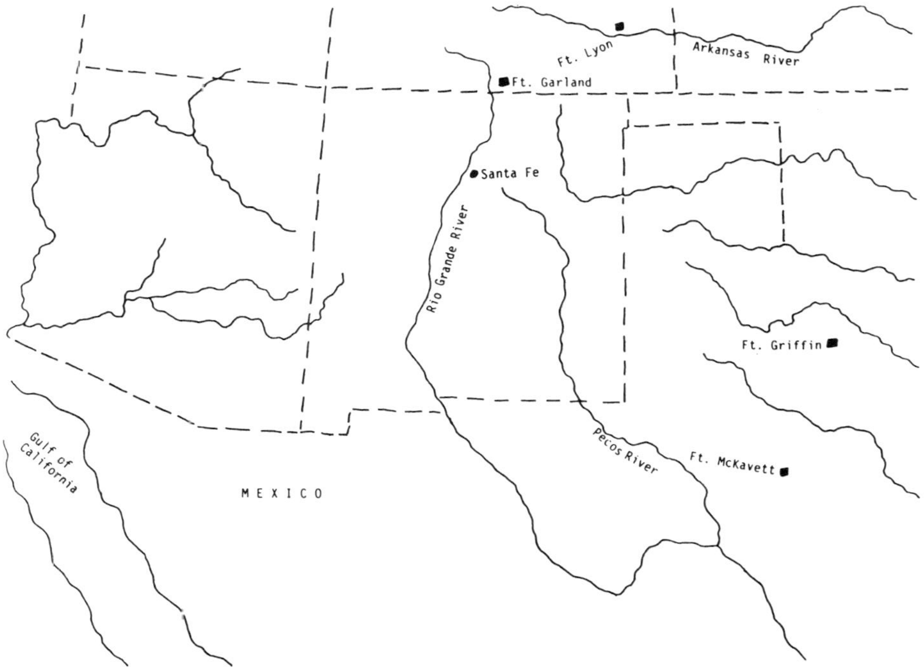

Chapter Two

LIEUTENANT JACOB KREPS ON THE FRONTIER: 1890–1898

Jacob Fordney Kreps was born in West Newton, Pennsylvania on October 22, 1860. During the Civil War, his father was a captain in the Seventy-seventh Pennsylvania Infantry, and four uncles had also served in the conflict.

Jacob Kreps' original ambition was to become a doctor; however, family pressures prompted him to make the army his career. The young man entered the Military Academy at West Point in 1879, and graduated with the Class of 1883.

A classmate wrote: "Jakey Kreps was a medium sized Pennsylvania gentleman—genial, cheerful, affable, and well liked by his classmates. Without quirks or erratic angles, he never bothered the Superintendent or clashed with the Commandant—but attended to his job diligently, and collected no more than a proper number of demerits. As to his scholastic standing, Kreps belonged to that large section of the class—aptly described as without ambition and devoid of fear...."

Upon graduation, Jacob Kreps was commissioned a second lieutenant in the Twenty-second Infantry, and remained assigned to the regiment throughout his thirty-five-year service career—leaving it only for three short tours of detached duty.

Colonel Kreps died in Pacific Grove, California on June 10, 1939, at the age of seventy-eight.

Jacob Kreps' fascinating story of his service with the Twenty-second Infantry begins in the summer of 1890. His account along with the records of

Captain Robert L. Hamilton and Captain William H. Wassell have been edited in the order that the events occurred.

During June 1890, the Twenty-second Infantry was split up between Forts Keogh, Buford, and Yates. In August, Lieutenant Kreps received orders to report to Fort Buford and was assigned to Company G.

Captain Hamilton wrote about the quiet summer: "The companies were not in the 'coffee cooling' business—even though it seemed that way.

"From time to time, detachments were sent out on scouting missions, or to agencies where the Indians were restless, and thought to be preparing to go on the warpath."

The peaceful garrison life came to an end during December, when Indian uprisings began to take place at the South Dakota agencies.

Company D was dispatched from Fort Buford under the command of Lieutenant John G. Ballance. The soldiers made a remarkable forced march to relieve a troop of Eighth Cavalry that was surrounded by a few hundred Sioux at Cane Hills.

Robert Hamilton reported the episode: "Lieutenant Ballance and his men started out on the evening of December 23 in a blinding snowstorm. By one o'clock on the morning of the 25th, the company had covered sixty-three miles. Ballance halted his column for a few hours to thaw out his half-frozen troops—then marched twenty-two more miles before meeting up with the cavalry. The Indians rapidly dispersed when they saw the foot soldiers."

Meanwhile, at Fort Keogh, Lieutenant Casey and his scouts were ordered to put down a Sioux revolt at the Pine Ridge Agency.

On January 7, 1891, Casey and his detachment were camped on the White River near Pine Ridge. Early that morning, several Sioux warriors entered the campsite and had a friendly talk with the lieutenant. After the conference, Casey and two of his scouts headed toward the agency. They had only walked a short distance, when Casey was suddenly shot in the back by the Brule warrior Plenty Horses.

Captain Hamilton eulogized the gallant soldier: "Lieutenant Casey was a brave and energetic officer—and an enthusiastic friend of the Indian. He originated the plan of organizing them into military companies—believing that by doing this, it would elevate and civilize them.

"Casey died before he had reached the meridian of his strength—

full of intellectual vigor and generous impulses. But, as most of us might wish to die—he did it in harness."

On January 21, 1891, First Lieutenant Jacob Kreps married Miss Helen Amelia Thompson of Meadville, Pennsylvania.

The young officer recalled what life was like for a new wife on an army post in the northwest: "A few years ago, a young lieutenant, shut up as he usually was in a remote frontier post, saved his pay and periodically 'went back east' to blow it on a good time.

"In those days, a practical girl was unknown in garrisons. Perhaps the journeys were too severe—a hundred odd miles of wagon travel being enough to discourage even the most enthusiastic lady in the 'hunt' for a husband.

"At any rate, the officer on leave seldom took to himself a wife. The dashing young warrior, devoid of sense of responsibility for anything but punctuality at drill, found frontier life as a bachelor very good fun—what with hunting Indians and antelope—and dancing with the guileless married coquettes at occasional garrison 'hops.'

"Therefore, the fledgling officer would swear to the girl of his heart that on the frontier every woman is queen. So, after a brilliant wedding, the new 'queen' set out to claim her throne.

"There was always a hearty welcome for the bride from the garrison officers and their families—small dinner dances in the honor of the newly married couple—a brief realization of romance—and then settling down to the cold facts.

"The young transplanted wife is now in a strange world. The very talk of her neighbors is to her a mysterious jargon of military technicalities. Even, when stationed near a town, few public amusements are possible on the salary of a lieutenant.

"Then the babies come, and there is always the awful 'servant question,' and the downright domestic drudgery—inevitable nowadays to all would-be homemakers.

"Sometimes weak health is added to the list of woes. But usually there is a sympathetic, helpful husband—for American Army officers are, as a rule, the most devoted, self-sacrificing family men in the world.

"The true test of an army wife is when the regiment takes to the road—in transit from one post to another. The troops usually march in two sections—preceding and following the wagons which carry women and children—the baggage wagons, with precious water kegs slung below the framework—and the long line of pack mules laden with forage. At night, the wagon containing each officer's personal effects is backed up against his tent.

"Drums beat reveille before dawn, and the army women, like quick-change artists, dress rapidly in the darkness—stick hairpins where they will do the most good—make quick connections between hooks and eyes—and as her husband lifts the canvas from over his wife's head, few toilet mysteries are exposed for the stars to wink at.

"A hasty cup of black coffee, settled by the stir of a charred stick—a sleepy climb into the wagons—a rapid journey until daylight—and then a halt for breakfast.

"On summer journeys across the great plains, hair and clothes become coated with alkali—and skin and lips crack and bleed. Officers and men cast aside the trim uniforms which lured their women from civilization, and wear simple flannel shirts and rough campaign trousers. The women appear in calico and gingham.

"Water cannot be spared for ablutions—every drop must be economized for the animals upon whose lives we depend.

"At sunset, after a long day's march, the column turns aside into the sagebrush. The water kegs are placed under guard. The army 'queens' bustle over the open fire—wrestle with the contents of Dutch ovens—burn holes in the front of their frocks—and blister their fingers on hot frying pans.

"Tinned meat, rice, tomatoes, and hot biscuits—washed down with black coffee, cause the trip to assume a more agreeable aspect.

"Soldiers, in the 'company streets' sprawl in the dust—chattering and card-playing. From the tents of the officers can be heard the merry prattle of gossip. Then the metallic sound of a banjo—and a soft tenor voice lifts in song, as the rising moon paints a silver glow across the desert.

"Out of all these experiences is evolved the typical army wife—who, before many years of service pass over her head, is trained by sharp discipline, reinforced by her own common sense, to be all things to all men.

"Her first duty as the wife of an officer of the United States Army is to make herself contented, no matter where her husband is stationed—in fine garrison quarters or a tent. And her second—if she fills the role of a hostess—is to provide something good to eat, and something strong to drink."

During the year 1891, the Cheyenne Indians at the Tongue River Agency became increasingly restless. In order to cope with a potentially explosive situation, the entire Twenty-second Regiment was assembled at Fort Keogh.

To further strengthen the army's position, a new campsite (Camp Merritt) was selected near the Tongue River. In December, Company A, commanded by Lieutenant W. E. Bruce, began erecting log quarters for additional troops. It was the coldest part of a severe winter, and the men worked under extreme hardship. Lieutenant Bruce contracted pneumonia from prolonged exposure to the vicious weather and died in February 1892.

By spring, the quarters at Camp Merritt were finally completed, and the garrison was changed every three months by companies from Fort Keogh.

On July 13, 1892, a telegram from Department Headquarters directed that all available companies of the Twenty-second Regiment be sent immediately to the scene of mining riots in the Coeur D'Alene region of Idaho. Early the next morning, Lieutenant Kreps' Company G and four other detachments were equipped for thirty days' field service and headed for the scene of the trouble.

For two weeks, the troops were actively engaged in maintaining order, guarding mines, and assisting with the arrest of leaders of the riot. After calm was restored, the soldiers returned to Fort Keogh.

During the next two years, the Twenty-second Regiment remained on garrison duty in the northwest—with only an occasional peacekeeping mission away from camp.

Then on Sunday, April 25, 1894, the regiment received urgent orders to intercept and arrest members of the Hogan division of Coxey's Army.

Captain Hamilton described the tense adventure: "The Hogan contingent of the unemployed had been organized in Helena and Butte, Montana. Their objective was to reach Washington and join the main corps of Coxey's Army. There had been incidents of trouble between these men and local authorities—but matters reached a crisis when the Hoganites seized a train of cars on the Northern Pacific Railroad, and completely blocked all traffic on the line. Mails were delayed for several weeks, and the entire northwest was paralyzed by a few hundred men.

"When the regiment received its orders, rumors had spread throughout the territory that the Hogan group were armed desperadoes—robbing and murdering peaceful citizens.

"Our instructions were to hold the regiment at Keogh, but have six companies ready to embark on a special train at a moment's notice. On the evening of the 25th, we received word that the Hogan division had arrived at Forsyth—about forty-two miles west of us. They were attempting to commandeer an engine from the roundhouse and continue their journey east.

"We were immediately directed to intercept the Coxey men before they could leave Forsyth. The troops were ready, and we scrambled aboard our 'special train'—a string of rickety, bouncing, swaying, wooden boxcars.

"It was to be a long remembered ride. We dashed at full speed over a single track stretch of road—headlong around dangerous curves—leaning one way then the other—unable to see what was ahead—and fearing any minute that the cars would jump the track and plunge down a ravine.

"At the other end of the iron rails, the desperate men were struggling with an engine—unaware of our order to stop them. If we did not reach Forsyth before the east bound train was off the siding, a collision was inevitable.

"However, just as the Hogan engine was ready to pull out, our train rushed in. The Coxey engineer was knocked from the cab, and about five hundred unarmed and unresisting prisoners were surrounded by a chain of soldiers.

"The Coxeyites were taken back to Helena where they were guarded by three companies until the end of July. The other detachments were assigned to protect bridges, tunnels, and trains."

In June 1896, the Twenty-second Regiment's long period of frontier service ended, and it was ordered to Fort Crook—near Omaha, Nebraska. The men were soon settled in fine new quarters. It was to be the longest unbroken period of garrison duty for the entire regiment since its organization.

There were practice marches and occasional encampments with the National Guard or G.A.R. Organizations. In July 1897, the regiment traveled to Chicago for the unveiling of the Logan monument.

However, the quiet contentment of peaceful army life soon came to an end. On February 23, 1898, news was received that the U.S.S. *Maine* had been blown up in Havana Harbor.

Chapter Three

THE CUBAN CAMPAIGN: THE SPANISH-AMERICAN WAR

The Spanish-American War is difficult to evaluate. In actual combat, the Indians at Little Bighorn killed almost as many American soldiers in one afternoon as the Spanish did during the entire conflict.

The real tragedy, however, was that, although the U.S. Army lost approximately 350 men killed in the Cuban campaign against the Spaniards, nearly 2,500 died from disease—malaria, yellow fever, typhoid, and dysentery.

As in all of its major wars, the United States found itself woefully unprepared. The entire army consisted of only 28,000 regulars—many of whom would still be needed at frontier posts to keep order in the far west.

The War Department itself lacked the organization for efficient mobilization. Military intelligence was another weakness. It was no secret that there were 200,000 Spanish soldiers stationed throughout Cuba—but their exact disposition was unknown—and there were no accurate maps of the country or its harbors.

Like all regular army units of this period, the Twenty-second Infantry had been brought up to a high state of efficiency and readiness. Most of the troops had had several years of service. They were a fearless breed of men, accustomed to being vastly outnumbered, and could be depended upon to fight to the last man.

After the *Maine* disaster, as the nation drew nearer to the outbreak

**Map 3.1
Cuba**

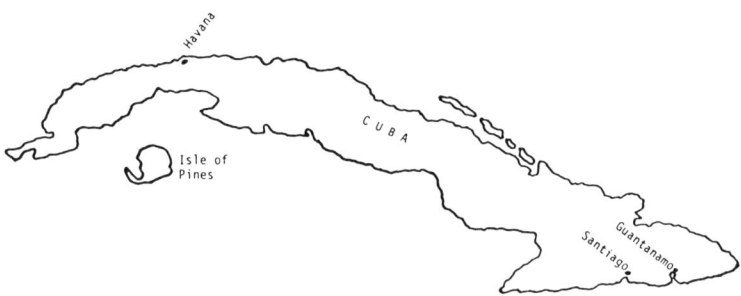

of hostilities with Spain, the Twenty-second Infantry quietly made preparations for war.

On April 18, 1898, the regiment, under the command of Colonel Charles A. Wikoff, departed Fort Crook by rail, en route to Mobile, Alabama. Twenty-nine officers and 484 enlisted men constituted the organization.

For more than a month after the incident at Havana, the newspapers of Hearst and Pulitzer had been screaming for revenge. Eloquent journalists quickly whipped the public into a frenzied fervor of patriotism. The battle cry "Remember the *Maine!*" echoed from New York to San Francisco.

At every stop, the troop train carrying the Twenty-second Infantry was greeted by enthusiastic citizens and brass bands. As the train lumbered south, decorative flowers were attached to the railroad cars. By the time the regiment reached Mobile, even the engine was covered with floral tributes.

Colonel Wikoff and his frontier soldiers arrived at the Alabama port on April 20, and camped near the city. For the next week, the troops engaged in drills, reviews, and inspections.

War was officially declared on April 25, and that same day, President William McKinley called for 120,000 army volunteers.

The order for volunteers was severely criticized by General William H. Carter: "The first promotions and assignments were made from experienced regulars—then followed a rush of applicants urged by Congressional delegations and those with official and social influence. The test of efficiency and experience was abandoned under this pressure, and appointments followed the usual lines of patronage. Although the matter was under the control of President McKinley, he gave in to spirited persuasion.

"There had been no well defined plan for organizing the army when called into active service. Brigades, divisions, and corps came into being through the expediency of the moment. A heterogeneous staff of volunteer officers were distributed among the regular army—and, in many instances, instead of being useful, they proved to be an encumbrance.

"In several cases, the generals in command detailed subordinate regular army officers to perform duties, while the volunteer officers had higher staff rankings and were unqualified for the same task."

On April 28, the Twenty-second Infantry received orders to break camp. They boarded a train for Tampa, Florida and arrived on May 2.

For the next few weeks, the monotonous and tedious days would be spent in drilling by company, battalion, and regiment.

Near the end of May, President McKinley issued a proclamation calling for 75,000 more volunteers. He had determined that the needs for a war with Spain would soon require a much larger military force than had been provided by the first call to arms. A great number of men would be needed for occupation duty in the Philippines, Cuba, and Puerto Rico.

While at Tampa, the Twenty-second Regiment was assigned to the First Infantry Brigade, Second Division, Fifth Army Corps. The First Brigade was comprised of the Twenty-second and Eighth Infantry Regiments, and was commanded by General William Ludlow. The division commander was General Henry Lawton. The entire Fifth Army Corps was under the command of Major General William R. Shafter and was ordered to assemble at the port of Tampa.

General Carter stated: "One of the most flagrant mistakes of the war was sending the whole army to Tampa, instead of eliminating the overcrowding by distributing the forces between Mobile and New Orleans. Hotel and railroad interests were the cause of this debacle."

General Shafter's corps was composed of 15,337 men—including nineteen infantry regiments, four light artillery batteries, two siege batteries, two companies of engineers, one detachment of signal corps, forty-eight troops of cavalry (dismounted), and a single hospital unit.

The Fifth Army Corps was almost entirely composed of regulars, with the exception of three regiments—the Seventy-first New York, the Second Massachusetts, and Teddy Roosevelt's Rough Riders.

Originally, the War Department plans called for the expedition to sail for Cuba in the fall—after the summer rains and yellow fever season. However, after Commodore George Dewey's decisive victory over the Spanish fleet at Manila Bay on May 1, public pressure demanded an immediate invasion of Cuba.

The need for troop-carrying ships became the number one priority. The army was finally able to charter about forty vessels. However, the ships were of all different sizes—and there were not nearly enough of them to transport the Fifth Army Corps, their horses, field artillery, and supplies.

Owing to the vast amount of work entailed in providing a large number of soldiers with complete equipment for foreign service—and then sending them hundreds of miles by water—many problems were encountered.

Supply trains were dispatched to Tampa as quickly as they were ready—but in no specific order. Within a few days, there were ten miles of loaded freight cars standing on a single track at Tampa without bills of lading or destination markings. The boxcars had to be broken open in a blind search for urgently needed items. There were no cranes dockside, and supplies had to be hauled aboard ship by hand. Mass confusion and chaos soon resulted as the wharves became clogged with cartons.

When Nelson A. Miles, commanding general of the army, arrived at Tampa on June 1, he was appalled at what he saw. Miles immediately realized that the army was not prepared for an active campaign in the tropics. The troops from northern posts were still wearing their winter uniforms. Because of delays in the army's supply department, summer clothing had never been shipped. The Twenty-second infantry was one of the units that was forced to wear their heavy uniforms throughout the Cuban action.

At first it was thought that each transport could carry a comfortable complement of troops. However, because of lack of space in the smaller vessels, it was necessary to pack the men in like cattle being shipped to market.

General Miles attempted to make room aboard the transports and still keep the essentials. He decided that the light artillery pieces could be handled by the soldiers. The artillery horses, many of the officers' mounts, and a large number of pack mules were ordered left behind.

On the morning of June 7, the Twenty-second Infantry Regiment broke camp and marched aboard the *Orizaba*. By afternoon, the entire Fifth Army Corps was on its assigned ships.

However, before most of the transports had hoisted their anchors, a report was received that Spanish warships had been spotted off the north coast of Cuba. The expedition was halted awaiting verification of the sighting.

(Although the false rumor of Spanish vessels probably was the principal cause for holding the troopships at Tampa, many authorities believed that the story was given out by Miles to buy more time for his men until they could be better supplied and equipped.)

The Fifth Army Corps sweated out the delay. More boxcars were unloaded and their contents packed away in the deep, dark holds of the transports. As to exactly which items were stowed aboard what ship—that was anybody's guess.

On June 10, a detachment of U.S. Marines landed at Guantanamo Bay, Cuba—and four days later General Shafter's corps sailed for Santiago.

Captain Henry C. Taylor, commander of the battleship *Indiana*, was the senior naval officer of the expedition. In addition, thirteen smaller naval vessels were assigned to escort the invasion force.

Four gunboats took the lead position as the transports left their piers. The troopships were formed in three columns according to their designated numbers.

Aboard the *Orizaba* (#24), the men of the Twenty-second Infantry packed the railings to watch the unforgettable spectacle. Lieutenant Kreps noted: "The scene presented by the embarkation was a memorable one—and was witnessed from the wharves by thousands of people who had been arriving at the port during the past twenty-four hours.

"As each vessel pulled out into the bay—with its hundreds of soldiers on deck and hanging from the rigging—regimental bands began to play, and cheers from ship and shore thundered for miles across the smooth, shiny water.

"The bay itself painted a picture difficult to describe. The line of troopships extended as far as the eye could see. Steamers and sailboats, both large and small, gaily decked with the nation's colors, frolicked about the transports and warships. Bright signal flags and bunting whipped from every mast. And that, along with the cheering and patriotic music, lifted the spirits of the weary soldiers. The waiting was over—we were off to war at last!"

The columns of the invasion fleet steamed a thousand feet apart—with an interval of six hundred feet between ships. Naval vessels were stationed on each flank of the transports, and two gunboats scouted the waters ahead.

As smoothly as the embarkation took place, the voyage had its disturbing moments. Navy Captain French Chadwick later wrote: "A potentially dangerous situation still existed. The transports were under army control, and did not come under naval direction until they sailed—and then only for convoy duty.

"Great difficulty was experienced through the wretched conduct of the civilian transport captains—who were under no proper control and wandered the sea at will. Hours were wasted in finding some of them.

"Everything connected with ocean transportation is a particular feature of maritime activity—and when the military is involved—of naval activity. Internal discipline of a ship, and proper control of her movements in a convoy, can only be insured by naval organization and naval command."

As the fleet steamed slowly toward Cuba, all vessels were darkened at night—with the exception of the *Seguranca*, which carried General Shafter and his staff. The rest of the flotilla was invisible to any Spanish ships that might be lurking nearby.

On June 17, the troops caught their first view of Cuba, as the Romano Keys, north of Puerto Principe, were sighted.

The expedition arrived off the Morro Castle entrance to Santiago Bay about noon on June 20. At that time, Colonel Wikoff was transferred to the Third Brigade, and Lieutenant Colonel John H. Patterson was placed in command of the Twenty-second Infantry.

The harbor entrance was surrounded by the blockade fleet of Admiral William T. Sampson. Trapped within the bay was the Spanish naval squadron of Admiral Pascual Cervera.

The transports formed in a column eight miles long and paraded across the front of the warships. Admiral Sampson's flagship, the *New York*, fired a salute, and each troopship dipped its flag as it passed the naval commander's vessel.

Shouts of welcome erupted from both the army and navy. The soldiers and sailors waved their hats and cheered, while the bands from both services created a din that could be heard up and down the coast.

The transports passed in front of the Spanish forts, and then circled out to sea—anchoring several miles from the Morro Castle.

That evening, General Shafter and Admiral Sampson held a conference aboard the *New York*, and invasion plans were finalized. Two landing sites were selected east of Santiago.

Before daybreak, the quiet tropical night was ruptured by the explosion of naval guns as the blockade fleet commenced bombarding several locations along the Cuban coast—including the towns of Daiquiri and Aguadores.

Captain Wassell wrote: "Daiquiri, seventeen miles east of Santiago, was the site chosen for the Twenty-second Infantry to disembark. There was an iron pier, five hundred feet long, and also a wharf. They had been used by a Spanish American company for unloading ore. The Spaniards attempted to destroy the pier by fire but were unsuccessful."

At noon, the order was given to disembark. However, many of the transport captains refused to bring their vessels close inshore.

Small boats from each troopship were lowered into the water and lined up in groups of six. Navy steam launches were directed to prepare for towing the troops to shore. Each launch was fitted with two tow lines, one on each side, and long enough so that one steamer could haul a dozen landing craft.

A strong wind was blowing, and there was heavy surf all the way to the beach. Several loaded boats capsized, throwing men and supplies into the water.

Wassell continued: "The regiment climbed into the boats and headed through the rough seas toward the smouldering dock. Enthusiasm ran high and rousing cheers burst from the transports still waiting to be unloaded. Regimental bands played—while out at sea, the navy bombarded the wooded mountains that rose from the beach. Shells whistled over our heads and exploded far up on the heights.

"The water seemed alive, as the little boats darted about like tiny bugs as they made countless trips between the troopships and the shore.

"Straining launches, pulling the boats packed with soldiers, puffed and whistled. Near the dock, a wall of surf roared an angry welcome—then broke in swamping torrents.

"Boats smacked against boats, and crashed against the pier—then thrown back by outgoing waves, they were flung forward again—someone finally grabbing a line tossed from the beach. The troops scrambled out, tossing blanket rolls ahead of them—but carefully handing rifles to helping comrades.

"Surf-drenched and panting, the men of the Twenty-second caught their breath—then cheered as the regimental colors were unfurled."

All afternoon, the invasion craft, packed to the gunwhales with Shafter's corps, traveled back and forth through the violent surf.

Artillery and supplies were loaded on barges; however, several of the flat-bottomed boats capsized while being hauled to the beach. Because of the rough water, some of the siege guns, part of the medical supplies, and vast quantities of provisions ended up on the ocean floor.

After a brief rest, the Twenty-second Infantry marched about four miles in the direction of Siboney and then camped near Daiquiri Creek.

Captain Carroll Dunham, division medical officer, described the march inland: "When the troops landed on the beach at Daiquiri, each man carried a blanket, poncho, and three days' rations rolled up in half of a shelter tent. However, as they trudged along the hilly trail, the choking dust turned to mud on their sopping wet uniforms.

"The ferocious sun bore down on the uncomfortable men and many threw away their blankets. It was not long before clothing and haversacks also began to litter the path. The scene looked more like a retreat rather than an unopposed advance.

"After we made camp, the soldiers began to regret what they had tossed away. The unbearable heat had passed, but the damp night air seemed doubly chilling after the exhausting march.

"Many of the men had abandoned their rations—and as there was no hope of a supply train reaching the camp before two or three days, the situation threatened to become serious.

"The troops pitched their tents on the sides or crests of hills—and as near running water as safety permitted. The soldiers had instructions to boil the water before drinking, but they had nothing in which to boil water except their tin cups.

"We were thus at the front, in the tropics, with our only food available being limited quantities of salt-pork and hardtack. Later on, while the men were suffering for want of vegetables, hundreds of barrels of potatoes and onions, that had spoiled aboard the transports, were heaved into the sea."

Before leaving Tampa, General Shafter loaded enough supplies for a six-month campaign for thirty thousand men and animals. He estimated that he had enough provisions to last his troops, their Cuban allies, the starving citizens of Santiago, and Spanish prisoners for at least three months. However, loss because of spoilage and difficulties encountered in transporting the supplies inland wreaked havoc with his plans.

While the Daiquiri landing was taking place, another amphibious operation was under way at Aguadores—three miles east of the Santiago Harbor entrance. These troops included Teddy Roosevelt's Rough Riders. A total of six thousand soldiers was landed the first day of the invasion.

An alert enemy might have taken advantage of the chaotic conditions to oppose the landings successfully. However, although the Spanish had six times as many troops in the area, they did nothing to prevent the Americans from coming ashore.

The following morning, the Twenty-second Infantry Regiment headed the advance inland and by noon had taken possession of Siboney. A Spanish force of six hundred had abandoned the location, offering no resistance. After entering the town, Company B captured the first enemy colors taken in the war.

The division medical detachment urged that every building in the captured villages be burned to prevent outbreaks of yellow fever. However, when the Twenty-second Infantry established their camp at Siboney, the quaint vine-covered cottages were seized for regimental headquarters and administrative offices. One of the first cases of yellow fever occurred at a house being used for staff headquarters at Siboney.

General Shafter remained aboard the *Seguranca*, supervising the unloading of men and supplies. General Joseph W. Wheeler was placed in command of all troops ashore. According to Shafter's orders, the corps was to dig in and establish a strong defensive position. Lawton's First Brigade was to take its station around Siboney so that the town could be used as a base of operations until troops and supplies could be assembled for the march on Santiago.

However, General Wheeler could not wait to get at the enemy. On the afternoon of the 23rd, he reconnoitered the jungle trail that led to Santiago, and decided to pursue the retreating Spaniards with General Sam Young's brigade of volunteers and a detachment of Rough Riders.

Wheeler's troops started out before daybreak and, about eight o'clock in the morning, ran into the Spanish rear guard at the village of Las

Guasimas. A fierce battle ensued, and the volunteers, who had been issued black powder cartridges, got their first taste of the Mauser rifle and smokeless powder. The Mausers left no tell-tale cloud to betray the enemy's location. While the Americans were blinded by their own rifle smoke, the Spaniards were able to key on the American position and directed their volleys accordingly.

Captain Wassell reported: "The Twenty-second Infantry was ordered in from outpost and sent to reinforce Wheeler's troops which were about four miles away. However, by the time we arrived, the action was over. That night, both outfits camped near Sevilla."

Shafter was upset with Wheeler, and ordered him to remain at Sevilla until reinforcements and provisions had arrived. The Fifth Army Corps commander was still aboard ship and having all kinds of trouble attempting to establish a forward base. The transports had been loaded haphazardly at Tampa—and unloading facilities at Daiquiri were practically nonexistent, but worst of all, the road inland was abominable. Jacob Kreps narrated: "Great difficulty was experienced in trying to move artillery and supplies. Although it was known in advance that the country was mountainous, and covered with a tangle of tropical undergrowth, a startling revelation awaited the troops as to the kind of roads that existed in southeastern Cuba.

"The main road from Daiquiri to Santiago is little more than a footpath—overgrown with vines and shrubs, and bristling with jagged rocks. The engineers had their work cut out for them trying to make the road passable, but the terrible heat made the task a nightmare.

"The so-called road through the jungle was choked with cactus, poisonous vines, and sharp high grass which cut exposed parts of the body like razors. The rays from the blistering sun caused the skyline of distant hills to quiver before the eyes as a strange gray mist floated upwards. While overhead, large vultures with outstretched wings methodically circled the marching men.

"The vegetation, cut down and trampled by our troops, rapidly began to ferment—giving off a sickening, sour smell. Thousands of gigantic yellow and red spotted land crabs wriggled and twisted along the sides of the path—their white claws clicking viciously at the feet of the soldiers.

"The heat became intolerable. The sun was like a giant yellow furnace—torturing every living thing—and turning every dead thing into grotesque shapes.

"The first heavy tropical rainstorm we encountered did not fall slantwise from the sky, but straight down. For three hours, the heavy, cold torrent poured from the clouds—drenching men to the skin, soaking blankets, and sending rivers of red mud and water racing down the narrow road.

"Only a short time earlier we had been sweltering with the heat—but then came one of the mysterious transformations of the tropics. The entire regiment began to shiver. Robust men could be seen shaking from head to foot—their faces turned ashen.

"Suddenly, hundreds of land crabs came clattering out of the jungle—squirming from underneath the poisonous vines and vegetation. The soldiers busied themselves crushing the swarming crabs under the heels of their boots. Every man who had quinine swallowed a dose.

"The officers, splashed with mud to their hips, hurried up and down the line, urging the men to strip off their clothes when the rain was over, and dry them over campfires.

"Presently, a few hundred men were standing about naked, while the hot sun turned the rain puddles to steam, and vicious tropical flies added to the misery."

For the next few days, General Shafter formulated his plan of attack. At first he believed that Santiago could be taken by siege, but quickly changed his mind. He received word that eight thousand Spanish soldiers, under the command of General Pando, had left Manzanillo with reinforcements and supplies for Santiago.

Other factors also contributed to the change in Shafter's plans. The city of Santiago was surrounded by high mountains that stood in ridges and ran practically parallel with the coast. Southeast of the city, on a hilltop, sat the village of San Juan—and three miles northeast was the town of El Caney. Both of these outposts had to be captured before any attack could be launched against Santiago.

On the morning of June 27, 1898, General Ludlow moved the Twenty-second Infantry forward about four miles on the El Caney road. The regiment remained there until the afternoon of June 30, when General Lawton ordered the entire division to resume its march north. That same day, Shafter went ashore and established his command post near the front—about a mile from the pickets.

The final plan agreed upon for the Santiago campaign was to send Lawton's division against El Caney—an action that was expected to take two hours. Then Lawton was to swing southwest to envelop the north flank of Spanish trenches and blockhouses on the San Juan Heights and Kettle Hill. The advance would also cut off Santiago from its water supply. The Cuban Insurgent leader, General Calixto Garcia, was asked to block the Cobre road and hold off any Spanish reinforcements.

The rest of the Fifth Army Corps would advance along the main road to Santiago and occupy the line of the San Juan River. They would then deploy and await General Lawton, who, having captured El Caney, would wheel to his left and form on the right of Shafter's First Division. All of these movements were to be completed by evening.

At three o'clock, Friday morning, July 1, Lawton's division was on the El Caney road—while Wheeler's troops, under General Sumner, headed up the valley to the hillside ranch of El Pozo. Sumner stationed Captain George Grimes' artillery battery three thousand yards from the San Juan Heights, and Captain Allyn Capron's battery on a bluff about a mile and a half from El Caney.

Lawton's orders were for complete silence as his men sneaked carefully up the narrow trail. The division commander's chief concern was his force being discovered by the Spaniards before the town could be surrounded.

As Lawton neared El Caney, he sent General Adna R. Chaffee's Third Brigade to encircle the high ridges on the north and east sides of the city. The First Brigade, with the Twenty-second Infantry in the lead, continued on the jungle path toward the south and west approaches to the town.

When Chaffee reached the crest of a ridge above El Caney, he looked down into the city. At its southwest corner was a steep hill—crowned by a stone fort. On the south and east sides of the formidable looking bastion, the Spanish had dug deep rifle pits and erected barbed wire fences.

To his right, Chaffee could see a long range of mountains—while to the left stretched the thick green jungle. In the distance, the red tiled roof of the Ducoureaud House loomed as a prominent landmark. The deserted estate was midway between El Caney and Santiago.

Around the perimeter of the town, the Spaniards had built several wooden blockhouses connected by trenches. These defenses were also protected by one or more rows of barbed wire.

Major General Breckinridge stated: "The Spanish blockhouse proved

Map 3.2
Santiago and El Caney Campaigns, July 1, 1898

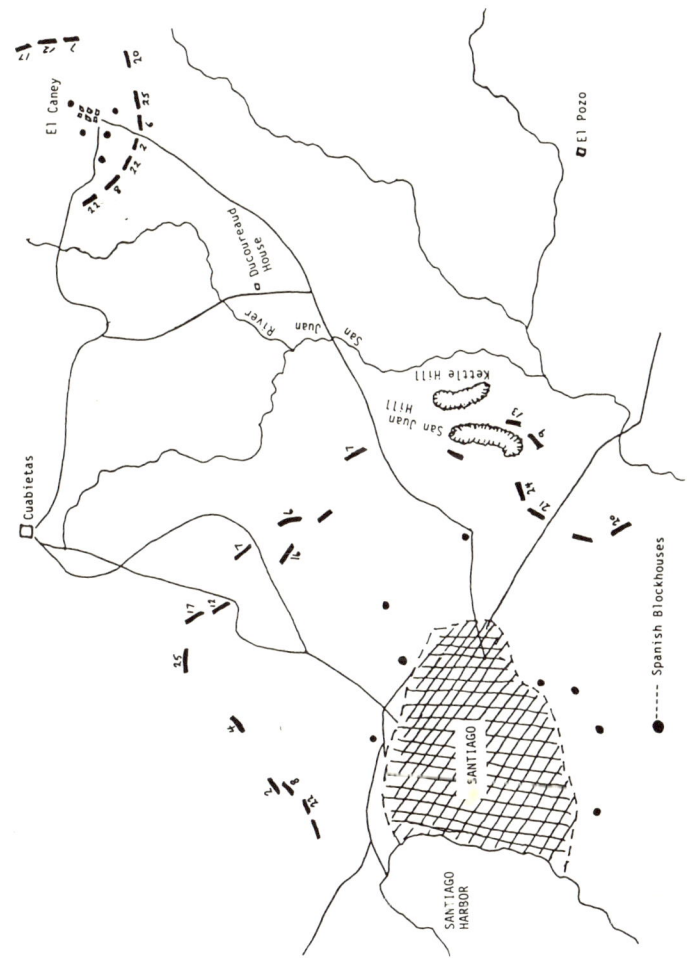

to be a more elaborate structure than the Americans had been led to believe. Its present arrangement had evolved over many years, and it was used in hostile territories to dominate the countryside at key locations and crossroads.

"The lower part of the blockhouse was usually built of masonry or wood, with a tall lookout tower rising from the center. A series of gunports were cut in the sides of the fortress—while at the top of the wall, a waist high parapet circled the building. This design gave the Spaniards two tiers of fire plus the spotter's post.

"The structure was surrounded by a series of trenches that were linked to the blockhouse. The trenches themselves were deep and narrow. The loose earth was thrown to the rear or side, so that the protection in front of the trench was solid ground. This type of stronghold was difficult to destroy—even by artillery fire. Many of the ditches were short, so that it was impossible to rake the rifle pits from one end to the other. Barbed wire was used freely in front of the trenches."

The Spaniards did not discover the Americans until sunrise, when Capron's battery opened fire. The report of the first salvo echoed and reechoed—then died away. There was no reply. More shots followed—still no answer from the enemy. It was not until the twenty-eighth barrage that the Spanish guns responded. Both sides then engaged in a hot artillery duel for about an hour.

Meanwhile, Captain Grimes' battery had commenced shooting at Spanish positions on the San Juan Heights. Moments later, the hilltops were obscured by clouds of yellow dust from the volleys. Enemy guns quickly retaliated, and for the next half-hour projectiles from both sides whistled through the damp air.

Shrapnel from exploding Spanish shells rained down upon Wheeler's infantry regiments and the Rough Riders. When the smoke finally settled, there were no Spaniards in sight—but there were hundreds of them concealed in trenches.

General Ludlow's First Brigade slowly approached El Caney. Captain Wassell described the action: "The Twenty-second Infantry led the advance along a trail overgrown with brush and vines until we reached the main Santiago-El Caney road near the Ducoureaud House. The Second Battalion was then deployed and skirmished northward through the jungle to check if there were any paths over which the Spaniards in the town might escape to Santiago.

"The First Battalion continued along the main road toward El Caney.

About a thousand yards from the city, Company A, our advance guard, came under sharp Mauser fire. The battalion rapidly deployed east and west of the road. Lieutenant Colonel Patterson was severely wounded by the sudden enemy attack, and Major Van Horne took over command of the regiment.

"The Second Massachusetts Volunteers, who formed the third regiment of Ludlow's brigade, had to be withdrawn from action early. Upon entering the main road, they were hit hard by long range volleys. On attempting to reply to the onslaught, the smoke from their Springfield rifles drew so much enemy fire that they were forced to retreat with heavy casualties.

"For more than a half-hour we cut through undergrowth and tangled vegetation, which was so dense that the battalion could not see more than ten feet to the front. In order to keep the line in order, men were continually forced to call out their position to skirmishers on either side of them.

"The Spanish barrage of bullets came from a chain of blockhouses and almost invisible rifle pits. At eight hundred yards a clearing was reached, and we got our first good look at the enemy's defenses. Our troops were ordered to lie down and take cover. In order to conserve ammunition, volleys by company and platoon were only fired during brief moments when the Spaniards showed themselves."

General Ludlow moved his command post to Company A and issued orders from that location for the remainder of the day.

After three hours of battle, the First Battalion had crept to within seven hundred yards of the enemy positions—suffering heavy losses in the process.

The dead and wounded were laid out alongside the road. The heat was intense and there was little shade. Hour after hour, the wounded lay unattended in the scorching sun—many slowly bleeding to death. The nearest medical station was about a mile to the rear, but the doctors were already swamped with walking wounded. There was no way that they could come to the aid of the more seriously injured.

Only six ambulance wagons had been allocated for the entire corps. Each division field hospital had shelter for about a hundred wounded. However, there were very few cots, mattresses, pillows, or blankets. Three dozen shirts were the only clothing available, and food consisted of beef extract.

Dr. Dunham described the scene as the wounded from El Caney

started to arrive: "By nine o'clock in the morning, the blood soaked men began to stumble in. We had five surgeons available, and they worked without interruption for twenty-one hours.

"By sundown, they had operated on more than a hundred and fifty soldiers. After that, the wounded came in so fast that it was impossible to keep records.

"During the day, the wounded rested on the grass, exposed to the tropical sun—by night they lay there damp and chilled. Our hospital had no lanterns. The surgeons worked by candlelight, and were subjected to the fire of Spanish snipers in the trees.

"Many of the wounded had gone into battle when the sun was at its zenith. They had thrown away everything except their rifles and ammunition—and wandered into the hospital half-naked. The first two days we cared for nearly eight hundred men.

"We originally believed that gunshot wounds produced by high velocity projectiles would be more destructive to life than our larger caliber shells. The reverse of this proved to be the case. The Spanish small-caliber Mauser bullet—which penetrates a yard of hard pine—goes completely through a man when it hits. The fact that the bullet makes its exit from the body does away with probing—a painful and dangerous procedure from which there is always the danger of infection—especially under the conditions of field surgery.

"At close range, the Mauser bullet generally rips the body in a perfectly straight line—and at such a rate of speed that it practically cauterizes the wound from its generated heat."

As the clock ticked toward eleven, General Shafter realized that the "two hour" battle for El Caney had now stretched to five and the outcome was still in doubt.

The situation was becoming serious. The First Division was still waiting patiently at the San Juan Heights for Lawton to join them for a combined assault on the fortified hills. In the meantime, they had been at the mercy of Spanish sharpshooters, and their losses were beginning to mount.

Shafter could not afford to procrastinate any longer. He would have to attack the heights without help from General Lawton's troops.

The Rough Riders were ordered out. They crossed the San Juan River and marched toward Kettle Hill. Lieutenant Colonel Theodore Roosevelt rode at the head of his men. To his right was the dismounted Tenth Cavalry.

There was no protective cover as the Rough Riders approached the smooth, open hillside. Enemy bullets and artillery swept the ground. Roosevelt realized that retreat was impossible. His troops would be picked off like flies. He hesitated for a moment—then shouted his orders, "Forward—charge!"

Pointing his sword in the direction of the Spaniards, Roosevelt led the way—and the Rough Riders dashed for the hill. The crack of the Mauser rifle was continuous. The colonel was a hundred feet in front of his men as they clambered up the steep slope. The wounded and dead dropped from the ranks, but others quickly took their place in the advancing line.

Astonished by the madness of the rush, the Spaniards stood up in their rifle pits for better aim. It was a fatal mistake—the Tenth Cavalry boys picked them off like ducks in a pond.

Forty yards from the enemy rifle pits, Teddy Roosevelt jumped from his horse, rallied his troops, and raced for the top of the hill.

When the Americans reached the summit, the Spanish deserted their trenches and ran. The position was won, but the Rough Riders had lost half their men—killed or wounded.

A quarter mile southwest of Kettle, General Hamilton Hawkins advanced on his objective—a blockhouse at the crest of San Juan Hill—surrounded by trenches and barbed wire.

Hawkins' command consisted of the Seventy-first New York Volunteers, and the Sixth and Sixteenth Infantry Regiments.

The first half-mile of the hill was wooded, and afforded some protection for the soldiers—but the last 1,500 yards was open slope. There would be no escaping the punishing fire from the blockhouse and trenches.

The Sixteenth Regiment was sent ahead as skirmishers. They were halfway across the dangerous terrain when the enemy attacked. General Marcus Wright described the action: "The Spaniards had waited until there was no chance for our men to get back under cover—then the enemy opened fire. The Seventy-first immediately dashed to the rescue. Spanish shrapnel exploded in their ranks, tearing holes four men deep in the line. Mauser bullets filled the air, but the boys never wavered. Ranks were filled as fast as they were ripped apart. Officers ran back and forth across the front, shouting at their men not to panic and keep moving ahead."

Lieutenant John Parker managed to get his battery of four Gatling guns across the San Juan River and rushed to the aid of Hawkin's beleaguered brigade. By the time the 71st Volunteers were within eight hundred yards of the blockhouse, Parker's machine guns were pumping 3,600 rounds per minute into the rifle pits.

The concentrated fire from the Gatlings kept the Spaniards crouched down in their trenches. The Americans, who were trapped on the hill, now broke into a run and raced for the top. The Sixth Regiment followed in support—men yelling and cheering as they sprinted headlong toward the enemy positions.

Company F of the Seventy-first New York was in the lead. Captain M. A. Rafferty's outfit fought their way to the crest of the bluff and—with bayonets fixed—charged the rifle pits—driving the Spaniards out into the open, and shooting them as they fled.

Company F occupied the blockhouse and trenches, but enemy artillery and Mauser fire from the next hill made the position untenable. Rafferty withdrew his men halfway down the slope and out of range. He then had his troops crawl on their bellies until they reached the Spanish left flank.

Other units of Hawkin's brigade sneaked around to the right and charged up the hill—driving the Spaniards from their trenches and into the deadly fire of Rafferty's company. The enemy tried to regroup and counterattack, but they were driven from the hills with heavy losses.

General Wright stated: "As our wounded were being carried from the battlefield, they were constantly fired upon by Spanish sharpshooters. The men who were helping the injured—and were under the protection of the Red Cross—were shot down without the slightest compunction by the Spaniards."

At Kettle Hill, most of the American casualties occurred during the deployment at the base of the slope, and not during the actual charge—which only took about nine minutes. At San Juan Hill, nearly all losses happened before the Gatling guns went into action and silenced the enemy fire while the troops rushed the Spanish trenches and blockhouse.

Meanwhile at El Caney, the Second Battalion of the Twenty-second Infantry, under the command of Captain B. C. Lockwood, was located to the extreme left of General Ludlow's line. The battalion received orders to hack its way through the jungle for half a mile, then swing east until they came to the Cuabietas road. This was to be their assigned position to block any enemy retreat from the town.

As Lockwood's troops cut their way through the heavy underbrush, they came under fire from Spanish snipers. The advance was so difficult that it was impossible to keep the formation together. Captain Robert Getty's company became separated from the rest of the battalion. They reconnoitered the area west of Lockwood's position, and succeeded in cutting the El Caney telephone line along the Cuabietas road. Getty rejoined the battalion at the edge of a fire-swept clearing, about five hundred yards from the trenches and main blockhouse.

Captain Wassell narrated: "The Spanish use of barbed wire proved to be very effective in stopping our advance. Wires were stretched near the ground to trip our men when they would run from one location to another. A few yards beyond, the Spaniards had constructed tall fences—strung with many lines of wire. These defenses were laid in cultivated valleys and other open spaces near the entrenchments. Enemy snipers were posted in the treetops around the clearings. Every fence compelled a momentary halt in our progress—and during those moments, we were exposed to pitiless fire.

"From noon until one o'clock there was a lull in the fighting, and men with wire cutters were ordered forward. Taking advantage of bushes and dips in the ground, they crawled to within two hundred yards of the trenches and cut many of the wires. They returned to our lines safely.

"Owing to the great extent of the front occupied by the regiment, General Ludlow moved the Second Battalion still farther to the west, and advanced the First Battalion to within five hundred yards of the enemy. The Eighth Infantry was positioned between the First and Second Battalions."

About one o'clock, the Spaniards increased their firing with renewed vigor. The Americans were forced to hug the ground at the edge of the clearings, and strain their eyes for moments when they could catch a glimpse of the enemy.

The fierce heat from the sun, beating down on Ludlow's brigade, was intolerable—and water was almost impossible to obtain. Any movement along the American line was sure to bring a well-directed volley from the Spanish rifle pits. Mauser bullets continually plowed the ground in front of the troops, plastering throat-choking dirt into their sweating faces.

The enemy was blessed with an unobstructed field of fire that covered Ludlow's entire position. The gunports and parapets of the blockhouses were slanted, so that even unaimed salvos would cover the clearing.

Jacob Kreps related: "Occasionally, the defenders stood upright in their trenches and parapets in order to fire volleys. At other times their rifle pits appeared dotted with straw hats—and a moment later, the enemy was invisible again. Our soldiers would shoot the hats to pieces but did not kill anyone. The Spaniards had resorted to the old trick of placing their hats on sticks for the men to shoot at.

"The blockhouse and trenches at the south end of town were protected by tall trees. Not only did they conceal the enemy's movements, but snipers stationed in the trees became a major problem. The sharpshooters could not be seen, however, their fire was devastatingly accurate."

Orders had been issued by General Shafter contemplating the effective use of artillery—but the assault by cannon fire never materialized. Because of the two-mile range of the high-powered Mausers, the American artillery was useless at close distances against the Spanish defenses.

Daring attempts were made during the day to move the gun batteries to within two thousand yards of the enemy lines, but the artillerymen were not able to load and fire their weapons under the blistering attack of Mauser bullets. They were forced to retire to the next available position in the rear—where they could barely see their objective.

However, the most frustrating aspect about the failure of artillery support was the fact that the gun batteries were unable to cover the infantry assaults on the San Juan Heights or El Caney adequately. This was because the gunnery officers could not distinguish the relative positions of either the Americans or Spaniards accurately enough to risk the danger of firing into their own troops.

General Wright stated: "On every hilltop surrounding the city of Santiago were blockhouses and trenches—about twenty of them. One of the most important of these defenses was at the foot of San Juan Hill on the banks of the river.

"While General Hawkins was attacking the Spanish positions on the bluff, Colonel Taylor's dismounted Ninth Cavalry was ordered to capture the riverfront blockhouse.

"Taylor's Second Battalion secretly took up their position in the jungle across the river from the enemy defenses. The First Battalion attempted to skirt around to the right. However, the companies became separated in the tall brush and lost sight of each other. After hacking through the undergrowth—and traveling about eight miles out of their way—they finally ended up on the right of the Second Battalion."

Spanish lookouts noticed the unusual movement across the river and opened fire into the dense foliage. The Americans did not return the volleys, but adopted Indian tactics—crawling silently through the underbrush and dodging from tree to tree—always advancing.

When Taylor's troops were within three hundred yards of the enemy trenches, they could see the Spaniards scurrying back and forth between the blockhouse and rifle pits. The Ninth Cavalry spread out as skirmishers and, taking careful aim, picked off any enemy soldier who showed his head. Occasionally, two or three Spaniards were observed trying to cut and run to the rear—but they were invariably gunned down. The unseen sharpshooters soon began to demoralize the Spanish defenders who commenced firing wildly into the jungle.

After their hard-fought victory at Kettle Hill, the Rough Riders and Tenth Cavalry arrived to support Taylor's brigade. The Ninth Cavalry moved out to flank the enemy on the left—between the newly arrived troops and the river. The entire American line then advanced through the thickest part of the brush.

General Wright continued: "The Spaniards were now able to spot our men darting through the tall grass and opened up with a heavy Mauser attack. One of the Americans suddenly let out with an old-fashioned rebel yell and others took up the cry all along the front. The unexpected clamor unnerved the enemy. Colonel Taylor shouted the order to charge and the troops dashed through the jungle. Whooping and hollering, they slid down the steep, muddy riverbank—splashed across the stream and raced up the opposite embankment—firing as they ran.

"The blockhouse was still a hundred yards away, but the Spanish could no more stop the rush than they could an avalanche. The enthusiastic, screaming Americans slashed across the trenches and busted into the blockhouse. The position was captured. Very few of the enemy escaped."

Meanwhile, the stalemate at El Caney was beginning to worry General Shafter. The Americans were holding their own, but the Spaniard's stubborn defense was inflicting heavy casualties on General Lawton's Second Division.

Shafter issued orders for Lawton to break off his attack on the town and join the First Division at San Juan Heights. However, Lawton realized that to comply with the directive at once would mean a demoralizing retreat in the face of the enemy. There was only one alternative—an immediate infantry assault on El Caney.

A plan of action was quickly formulated. General Ludlow's brigade would rush the south side of the town, while Chaffee's men would storm the stone fortress. Two additional regiments were summoned from the Ducoureaud House to support Ludlow's attack.

Capron's battery opened the offensive with a rapid fire barrage from short range. Shell after shell battered the fort—blasting jagged gaps in its masonry walls.

About two o'clock, General Chaffee gave the signal to charge. His troops raced across the ravine that skirted the east side of the town and swarmed up the fortified hillside. With fixed bayonets, they scrambled through the barbed wire fences and sliced their way across the trenches. Fleeing Spaniards, trying to escape, were shot as they ran.

Captain Arthur Lee reported: "When the hill was taken, everyone acted as if the battle was over. The troops jumped around like schoolboys—cheering and waving their hats, while officers shook hands and congratulated each other.

"It slowly dawned on us, however, that we were an easy mark for somebody. Bullets began splattering against the walls of the fort and several men were hit. It quickly became apparent that, although we held the hill, the enemy still owned the town. We made a generous target for the Spaniards. Our soldiers rapidly spread out around the fortress, and opened fire on the blockhouses and trenches from above."

At the same time that Chaffee's troops were assaulting the hilltop, Ludlow's brigade—led by the Twenty-second Infantry—rushed from their jungle cover and sprinted across the fire-swept clearing.

Yard by yard, trench by trench, and blockhouse by blockhouse, the First Brigade fought its way into the town. The Spanish garrison was besieged on all sides. The enemy became confused and disoriented. They searched for a route to withdraw their forces to the safety of Santiago, but there was only one path still open—the Cuabietas road.

Captain Lockwood's Second Battalion had been waiting all afternoon to get into the fight. They could hear the battle raging, but had no idea of the outcome until Spanish soldiers were seen fleeing toward them.

Very few, if any, of the enemy escaped Lockwood's ambush. More than two hundred dead and wounded were counted along the intended retreat route.

Captain Wassell recalled the moment of triumph: "We heard shouting from the hill. At first we did not comprehend the reason for the celebration—but as the sounds rose in volume, we realized that they were American voices cheering their victory.

"The stone fort, with its trenches cut in solid rock, had fallen. Chaffee's brigade had sliced through the wire entanglements and stormed the bastion. Where all morning the Spanish colors had waved, now appeared the flag of the United States."

About four o'clock all firing had ceased, and the Americans were in complete possession of the town. The Fifth Army Corps casualties for the one-day battle at San Juan Heights and El Caney totaled 200 dead and nearly twelve hundred wounded. The Twenty-second Regiment was saddened by the news that Colonel Wikoff had been killed earlier in the day at San Juan Hill.

General Ludlow eulogized his troops: "The commander of the Second Brigade wishes to congratulate the officers and men of this unit on the gallantry and fortitude displayed by them in the investment and capture of El Caney.

"Infantry attacks on well defended and fortified positions are recognized as the most difficult of military undertakings, and are rarely successful. The enemy defense was conducted with admirable skill behind an elaborate system of blockhouses and trenches. Nevertheless, after a stubborn and bloody battle lasting nearly nine hours, the town was captured and its garrison virtually annihilated.

"This action will take its place as one of the conspicuous events in military history, by reason of its success under extremely difficult conditions. All who contributed toward the achievement warrant present and future congratulations."

The weary warriors of the Twenty-second Infantry had hoped for a good meal and a few hours' rest—but it was not meant to be. During the early morning march to El Caney, the troops had been ordered to stack their haversacks and blanket rolls at different locations along the road. The belongings were placed under guard. However, a few hours later, when the walking wounded began straggling to the rear, the surgeons called upon the sentries to help bring the injured men to the aid station. Two miles of blankets, ponchos, and rations were left unguarded, and anyone who passed along the trail helped themselves to whatever they happened to need.

After the conflict, when the regiment returned to pick up their belongings, very little was left. About six o'clock, rain started to fall, and the dead-tired soldiers—without having eaten, and no blankets or ponchos to keep themselves dry—laid down alongside the muddy roadway—and slept.

Jacob Kreps wrote: "Picket firing was constant throughout the night. All spare men were engaged in burying dead—both American and Spanish—and hauling the seriously wounded to the field hospital at Siboney. The journey was made in army wagons which bounced and jolted over stones and ruts for nine excruciatingly painful miles."

At three o'clock the following morning, July 2, Lawton's division was ordered to head for Santiago. His brigades were harassed by snipers during the march, but managed to reach their assigned positions on schedule. The string of American trenches stretched in a five-mile horseshoe curve around the city. The Twenty-second Infantry dug themselves in on the extreme right of the line.

Throughout the day, Ludlow's troops sandbagged rifle pits in anticipation of an enemy assault. At 10:30 that night, the Spaniards launched an artillery barrage and infantry rush against the right flank of the Second Division. The Twenty-second Regiment held their ground and beat back the enemy charge.

General Breckinridge commented on the Spanish attack: "During the fierce fight there were a great number of casualties resulting not entirely from aimed fire, but from bullets clearing the crest of our trenches and striking men as they were moving up into position—or rushing back and forth carrying water and caring for the wounded.

"Many injuries also resulted from the fire of snipers stationed in the trees. It seemed incredible that men could be so reckless as to remain within our lines and continue shooting. Other officers believed that, what was reported to be sniper fire, was simply spent bullets skimming over the top of our breastworks. But I, and members of my staff, can testify to the fact that the sharp crack of the Mauser rifle could be heard close to us—and there was every indication that selected aim was taken against individual soldiers.

"Scouting parties were sent out from time to time to get a hold of these fellows, and a number of them were captured or shot. It was not until a few days later, however, that the woods were cleared of these sharpshooters."

About nine o'clock on the morning of July 3, heavy gunfire was heard south of Santiago and continued for several hours. Repeated rumors confirmed the fact of a naval engagement, and all along the line, Shafter's troops anxiously waited for the results. Captain Wassell stated: "Meanwhile, depressing news was spreading across our front—the Spanish warships had broken out of Santiago Harbor and destroyed the American blockade vessels. Rumor followed rumor—first one fleet then the other had been sunk.

"Finally we began to hear the same exuberant cheering that gladdened our hearts at El Caney. It began very faint at first and far to the left—then taken up regiment after regiment, ever louder, until at last it reached the Twenty-second Infantry—a mighty celebration of our Navy's victory. Men whistled, shouted, waved their hats and flags, and danced in the trenches. Regimental and shipboard bands blared forth with 'The Stars and Stripes Forever' and other patriotic marches."

With the Spanish fleet no longer a threat Santiago could be shelled from both land and sea. About noon, General Shafter sent a message to the commander of the Spanish garrison, General José Toral, that unless he capitulated, the American Army and Navy would bombard Santiago.

Toral replied that he would not surrender the city. However, in the interest of humanity, Shafter sent word back that he would postpone the attack until noon of July 5.

Shafter wrote: "I did not wish to fire on a city filled with women and children if it could be avoided. I also knew that most of the people within the town were our friends.

"Small groups of refugees had been continually fleeing Santiago from the time we reached Sevilla, and most of them were now congregated at Siboney."

Dr. Dunham recorded the tragic set of circumstances that were about to occur—and would take more American lives than the war itself: "When the notice of the bombardment was sent to General Toral, the city gates were opened and thousands of miserable inhabitants rushed out toward the invading corps. They were received with compassion and kindness—which did more credit to the hearts of our men than to their heads.

"The rabble were hungry, and stricken with disease and infection. They were truly more menacing to the Americans than all the soldiers of Spain.

"The sickly refugees mingled with our friendly troops, and packed the unburned villages of El Caney and Siboney. Incredible as it may seem, the few ambulances we had available were used to haul the civilians—many of whom were fever stricken. And these same ambulances also carried our own sick and wounded.

"There had been hushed mutterings of yellow fever during the campaign—but immediately after the residents of Santiago flooded into our lines, the trouble began. First a few cases—then twenty—then two hundred—and the count kept climbing."

The chief surgeon of the volunteer regiments, Lieutenant Colonel Senn, stated: "I was more than astonished when I arrived at Siboney on July 7, to find that thousands of refugees from infected districts were allowed to enter the camps unmolested and mingle freely with our soldiers.

"Our troops were in a strange land among strange people. The Americans enjoyed the novelty of hero worship—not realizing how dearly they would be called upon to pay for such a privilege. Houses and huts in which yellow fever was raging were visited regularly, and the dangerous germs of this and other diseases were inhaled as a matter of course.

"The results of such intimate association by our susceptible soldiers with the natives could be readily foreseen. It required only the usual time for the disease to make its appearance. And when it did so, it was everywhere along the line of entrenchments."

General Wright reported: "The city of Santiago was on the verge of starvation. Only rice and black bread were obtainable, and these were doled out in small quantities by the town officials.

"Spanish army deserters stated that General Toral could not hold out much longer, and that public opinion was overwhelmingly in favor of capitulation."

The countryside for miles around soon became dotted with refugee camps. In El Caney alone, three thousand people packed the town. Other hungry, barefoot refugees plodded toward Siboney. The sick were carried on litters, but the so-called road was so rugged and the heat so unbearable that many of them succumbed to the hardships of the journey.

While the men of the Fifth Army Corps sweated out the surrender negotiations, they busily decorated their rifle pits with American and regimental colors. Throughout the day, large white flags of truce continually crisscrossed the open field between the opposing trenches.

On the morning of July 4, the Twenty-second Infantry was ordered into position three miles farther to the right and closer to the besieged city.

By mutual agreement, peace talks were extended until four o'clock on the afternoon of July 10. However, no progress was made, and the Spaniards opened a three-hour artillery barrage on the American lines. The next morning, the U.S. Navy commenced their bombardment of Santiago. The city was not visible from the ships, which had to stand offshore far enough to enable them to fire over the protecting range of hills. The only real damage to the town occurred when one of the naval shells struck a church that was being used as an ammunition supply dump.

Jacob Kreps wrote: "Our artillery and siege guns began blasting the Spanish positions. General Shafter considered launching a frontal infantry assault on the enemy trenches. But as we were preparing for the charge, the sky became overcast and visibility became poor—even the mountain tops were covered.

"Vivid flashes of lightning and the deep roll of thunder, reverberating across the hills, gave alarming notice of the impending storm. The wind picked up force, and choking clouds of dust covered both us and the enemy. Then the rain flooded down from the sky.

"After fifteen minutes, the downpour subsided and our guns resumed their attack. It was one of the most one-sided artillery duels ever seen. The field guns, mortars, and Gatlings pitilessly pounded the Spaniards. The enemy return fire was weak and their aim was poor.

"The American trenches were elaborately protected by more than twenty thousand sandbags—while the Spanish were compelled to build barricades using bamboo poles filled with earth. Gunports were cut in the ramparts, but the Gatling guns virtually sliced the wood to splinters."

During the night, the Twenty-second Regiment was moved forward to the northeast point of Santiago Bay—less than two hundred yards from the enemy rifle pits. Captain Wassell stated: "We were so close to the Spaniards that we could yell at each other. Some of our men could speak Spanish, and many verbal exchanges took place—usually ending in mutual cursing."

However, the lengthy siege was beginning to take its toll on the Fifth Army Corps. General Marcus Wright observed: "The men had been spending day and night crouched in the trenches—often knee-deep in water from thunderstorms, and always on short rations.

"The oppressive heat and sickness were having a detrimental effect on the troops. They were unprotected from the drenching rains, and fell easy prey to tropical diseases. Morale was low, and every day it became more difficult to arouse them to vigorous action."

General Nelson Miles arrived in Cuba on July 8. On the way to the front, he passed through Siboney and saw that the village had not been set afire. He issued immediate orders to burn down the disease-ridden houses. The occupants were given fifteen minutes to get out—and then only with the clothes on their backs.

When Miles reached the American positions, he held a quick conference with General Shafter. Maps of the Spanish fortifications were consulted, and plans for a quick end to the siege were discussed. Because of the climate, and the sick and weakened condition of the American troops, both generals agreed that it was absolutely necessary for Santiago to be taken as soon as possible.

Shafter drafted a letter to General Toral demanding the unconditional surrender of the city—stating that the defeat of the Spanish garrison, with great loss of life, was only a matter of days.

The following morning, Toral sent a messenger to Shafter proposing a meeting. A parley was immediately arranged midway between the Spanish and American lines—underneath the shade of a large cottonwood tree.

This time Generals Shafter, Miles, and Wheeler met face to face with General Toral and his aide, Colonel Valasquez. All previous negotiations had been conducted through intermediaries.

Shafter repeated his terms, which were agreed to in principle by Toral, but the Spanish commander said that he would have to obtain permission from Madrid, and requested a few days' grace period. This was agreeable to the Americans.

General Miles believed that the acceptance of any reasonable terms for the capitulation of the city was preferable to a long, drawn-out siege: "The surrender of Santiago would give us a harbor for use by the fleet, and the city as a base of operations. The property of foreign residents would be saved. And the thousands of refugees, now being fed and cared for by our army, would be able to return to their homes."

Another reason for the expedient end to hostilities was the continued difficulty in landing supplies at Daiquiri and Siboney. The frequent violent rainstorms made it virtually impossible to send boats and barges to shore. In the meantime, the troops were barely existing on half-rations—and the need for medicines and bandages was critical. With

Santiago in American hands, the transports would have dock and wharf facilities, and could unload in a protected harbor.

For the next couple of days, surrender details were hammered out by negotiators from both sides, and on July 16, the final terms were agreed upon. Among the conditions:

> The American Hospital Corps was to attend to all sick and wounded Spanish soldiers.
>
> The guns and defenses of Santiago were to be turned over to the Fifth Army Corps in good condition.
>
> The Spanish garrison troops were to be returned to Spain as soon as possible aboard American transports.
>
> The Spaniards also agreed to cooperate with the Americans in destroying mines at the harbor entrance and in the bay.

At nine o'clock the following morning, General Shafter and his staff marched to the cottonwood tree where Shafter sent word that he was ready to take possession of the city.

A short time later, General Toral, accompanied by his officers, arrived. The two generals saluted each other, and salutes were also exchanged by the officers of both sides.

The Santiago commander's voice trembled as he spoke in Spanish: "Through fate I am forced to surrender to General Shafter of the American Army the town and strongholds of Santiago."

Shafter humbly replied: "I receive the city in the name of the government of the United States."

After the documents were signed, the Spaniards snapped to attention and presented arms. General Shafter and his officers mounted their horses and headed for the city gates—followed closely by the Second Cavalry and Ninth Infantry Regiment.

When the troops along the American front noticed Shafter and his detachment moving forward, the victory celebration began. Boisterous cheering and the waving of hats spread like a forest fire along the miles of trenches.

As Shafter and his men neared Santiago, they witnessed the devastation caused by the siege. James Archibald, of the San Francisco *Post*, described the approach to the city: "All along the road were carcasses of horses and shallow graves that had been scratched open by vultures. The odor was nauseating.

"The first barricade we encountered was a cleverly conceived barbed wire entanglement. It did not close the roadway, but compelled anyone entering to zigzag back and forth. Next came sand-filled barrels protecting the trenches. Side streets were blocked by paving stones with openings for gunports. The thick walled houses were also holed for riflemen."

General Shafter stated: "It would have cost five thousand lives to take the city by assault."

The Americans moved cautiously through the quiet avenues that led to the Governor's Palace—which fronted on the Plaza de Armas, a small park in the center of town. At the other end of the square stood the city's cathedral.

The air was filled with tension as Shafter's troops entered the plaza—now packed with three thousand spectators. Cheers suddenly broke out from American sympathizers. A few fist fights developed, but were quickly stopped by the police.

General Shafter and his officers were greeted at the palace steps by the mayor of Santiago, Gabriel Ferrer, and about fifty minor city officials. A cold lunch was served within the building for all the dignitaries.

By this time, every house and rooftop surrounding the plaza was jammed with onlookers—and people still continued to push their way into the already overcrowded square.

A few minutes before noon, Lieutenant John Miley was sent to the roof of the palace—an American flag in his hands. The Fifth Army Corps commander and his staff, followed by the Spanish delegation, proceeded outside to view the ceremony.

Miley attached the Stars and Stripes to the flagpole halyards, and as the cathedral bell sounded the first stroke of twelve o'clock, he hauled the flag to the top of the mast. The people removed their hats and the soldiers presented arms. When the last chime of the hour tolled, a military band struck up "The Star Spangled Banner," and Capron's artillery battery, from two miles away, fired a twenty-one gun salute.

Shafter's troops, who had been standing at attention in the plaza, could not contain their excitement any longer. They burst out into a frenzy of shouts and hat waving. The crowd also got caught up in the revelry—and soon practically everyone was cheering and yelling "Viva los Americanos!"

However, this was nothing compared to the festivities taking place at Fifth Army Corps rifle pits. Jacob Kreps described the joyous scene: "The Twenty-second Infantry and their band paraded in perfect formation along the battlefront. As far as the eye could see, soldiers were jumping about on the crests of the trenches, celebrating their hard fought victory. The surrounding hills were alive with frolicking troops—and brightly colored regimental and American flags dotted the landscape.

"Individual companies praised and congratulated each other. One of the Rough Riders called for three cheers for Colonel Roosevelt. The response was soul-stirring and a mighty roar filled the air. The colonel was noticeably moved. He doffed his hat and bellowed out for three cheers for General Shafter and the army."

After the ceremony, Shafter and his staff returned to the American lines, leaving a detachment of soldiers on patrol duty within the city.

As soon as the United States flag was observed flying from the Governor's palace, a steady stream of refugees began jamming the roads on the way back to their homes. At the same time, Spanish soldiers marched out from Santiago and camped near the American lines. The Spaniards chatted amiably with the conquering troops, who shared their sparse rations with the former enemy.

Throughout the afternoon, the waters of the bay were cleared of mines, and about five o'clock, the steamer *State of Texas*, carrying nurses and medical supplies, entered the harbor. Other transports followed, packed with provisions for the hungry soldiers of both sides.

Immediately upon reaching field headquarters, General Shafter issued orders for the Fifth Army Corps to prepare to break camp, and move to the ridges and higher elevations where living conditions were healthier.

Jacob Kreps stated: "On the following day, July 18, the regiment was moved back to San Juan Heights. Everyone was suffering from unavoidable exposure. During the daily thunderstorms, the men had only been able to get slight protection from their shelter halves. For many days and nights they had worn the same wet clothing and slept in water-filled trenches. Malaria, yellow fever, typhoid, and dysentery spread through the regiment until only a few officers and a small number of men were fit for duty—and these only because they were less sick than the others."

(By the time the Spanish surrendered, barely ten percent of Shafter's corps was healthy enough to continue the siege. It was fortunate that this fact was kept from the enemy; otherwise it is doubtful that the Spaniards would have capitulated.)

Siboney was selected to be the central location for yellow fever cases. The field hospitals in the hills had to be abandoned, since the rains had made the jungle so wet that it became uninhabitable.

Cuban railroad cars were spotlessly cleaned and brought to the village. Hospital tents were also erected, but there was still a shortage of medicines.

There were so many sick men camped in the hilly countryside that efforts to nurse them were futile. Within a week, more than a thousand cases of yellow fever, malaria, and typhoid had been packed into the hospital compound—with more arriving every day.

Siboney was placed under quarantine and completely isolated from the rest of the corps. The dispatch boat *Anita* managed to bring a load of badly needed ice to the hospital, but no medicines—not even an aspirin.

In order to break high fevers among the sick, the doctors prescribed laxatives and diuretics. The men were told to drink plenty of water, but were not allowed anything to eat.

(It was not until 1901 that Dr. Walter Reed, U.S. Army, isolated the yellow fever germ and identified the mosquito as the carrier of the disease.)

No matter how hard the medical department worked to save lives, the soldiers continued to succumb to the tropical illnesses at an alarming rate.

General Shafter held a meeting with his division and brigade commanders. It was unanimously decided that the only salvation for the troops was to leave Cuba as soon as possible. The regiments would be replaced with men from southern states—who were thought to be immune to yellow fever.

The Surgeon General selected Montauk Point, New York as the campsite for the returning American soldiers. It was located at the extreme eastern end of Long Island and thought to be far enough away from populated areas for safety. The receiving station was named Camp Wikoff in honor of the Twenty-second Infantry's popular colonel.

THE SPANISH-AMERICAN WAR 51

As the American troops boarded the transports for their trip back to the United States, they were issued their summer uniforms—just in time for the sharp sea-breezes and chilly nights at Montauk Point.

The first steamer to leave Cuba, the *Seneca*, arrived at New York on July 21 with 100 sick and wounded. Dr. Dunham described the outrageous journey: "The *Seneca* was a small vessel—not a hospital ship. Taking up space that could have been used for additional soldiers, were fifty non-military passengers—including newspaper correspondents and attaches of foreign governments. The ship's captain protested carrying civilians, but to no avail.

"Two young surgeons and one Red Cross nurse were assigned to care for the patients. The nurse attempted to get medical supplies from the *State of Texas*, but she was only able to obtain a small quantity of medicine, beef tea, and malted milk. The soldiers were carried to roughly constructed bunks down in the stifling-hot cargo hold of the vessel.

"During the voyage, the *Seneca* ran short of ice. And only a portion of the water needed for the sick was able to be produced by the ship's condensers. Wounds were washed with sea-water.

"The weather was stormy and the ocean extremely rough. The vessel pitched and rolled—tossing the injured and feverish men from their bunks. Partly healed wounds opened up and started to bleed—but there was nothing to rewrap them with. The civilian passengers ripped up their shirts and skirts for bandages. The doctors were forced to operate with pocket-knives, since there were no surgical instruments on board."

When the *Seneca* finally reached port, the local quarantine officers would not let the troops be unloaded until it was determined if there were any yellow fever cases among the sick. No temperature charts were kept during the voyage because there was not a single medical thermometer on the entire ship.

The *Concho* left Cuba on July 23 with 172 sick and wounded. Not only was this vessel overcrowded, but the one doctor on board was also ill. Because of the shortage of medical supplies at Siboney, none could be spared for the *Concho*.

However, things were not much better at Camp Wikoff. The carpenters, constructing hospital and barrack buildings, went on strike for higher wages—and refused to work in the rain at any price.

The arriving fever-ridden soldiers were required to sleep on the ground, with nothing to eat except the army rations they had brought with them. According to regulations, the troops could not be allowed any additional food until they had finished all the rations that had been requisitioned.

(In contrast to the struggle for existence at Montauk Point, barracks were built in a few days at Portsmouth, New Hampshire—in preparation for receiving 1,100 Spanish Navy prisoners captured when their fleet was destroyed off Santiago on July 3.)

General Ludlow's brigade, including the Twenty-second Infantry Regiment, was notified on August 11 that they were to return home aboard the *Mobile*. The troops were inspected by medical officers for signs of yellow fever. All infected clothing was burned, and summer uniforms issued. The brigade embarked on August 13.

Jacob Kreps wrote: "The journey from Cuba to the United States added more hardships to the regiment's already long list. No provisions had been made for the sick. Men suffering from fever, chills, and various stomach ailments, were compelled to eat ordinary rations. Eleven deaths occurred during the trip.

"We reached Montauk Point on August 20. But by now the news of the dreadful campaign, and the appalling stories of the ocean voyages, had reached the American public. Privations were now a thing of the past. The people seized every opportunity to load upon the returning soldiers all the delicacies of life. Nothing was left undone, by the government or private citizens, that could add to the comfort—even luxury—of the troops. And although the majority of the men were prevented by sickness from enjoying the many good things thrust upon them, the kindness prompting these gifts cheered more than one invalid to recovery."

On September 16, the Twenty-second Infantry left Camp Wikoff for its former station—Fort Crook, Nebraska. Out of the 513 officers and men who had left the post four months earlier, only 165 returned—and almost all of those were still suffering from disease and malnutrition.

Upon the Twenty-second's return to Nebraska, four additional companies were authorized—bringing the regimental strength to twenty-six officers and 1,070 enlisted men. Jacob Kreps was advanced in rank to captain and appointed commanding officer of Company M.

However, nearly the entire regiment was now comprised of new recruits. It would take four months of intensive training before the Twenty-second Infantry would be prepared to be sent into action again.

Chapter Four

THE BATTLE OF MANILA

In the latter part of April 1898—a few days prior to the outbreak of hostilities between the United States and Spain—E. Spencer Pratt, the American Consul General at Singapore, conceived a plan whereby a Philippine revolutionary by the name of Emilio Aguinaldo would return to the islands.

Aguinaldo was the leader of a secret nationalist society called the Katipunan. The organization had battled Spanish rule in the Philippines for several years. In 1896 an armistice was reached that granted the Filipinos freedom of the press, certain governmental posts, and an indemnity of 800,000 pesos—in return for which the leaders of the rebellion were to leave the islands. The indemnity, theoretically, was to recompense widows and orphans—and those who had lost their property during the rebellion.

Emilio Aguinaldo and forty of his lieutenants traveled to Hong Kong, where Aguinaldo cashed a draft for 400,000 pesos and put it in a bank for the purpose of buying arms to finance another revolution in case the Spanish did not live up to their part of the bargain.

After Commodore George Dewey defeated the Spanish fleet at Manila Bay on the first of May 1898, he occupied the enemy's naval facility at Cavite and cut the ocean telegraph cable. Manila was now cut off from daily contact with Spain.

However, Dewey also had a problem with communications. His only thread to the outside world was a small dispatch boat, the *McCulloch*,

**Map 4.1
The Philippine Islands**

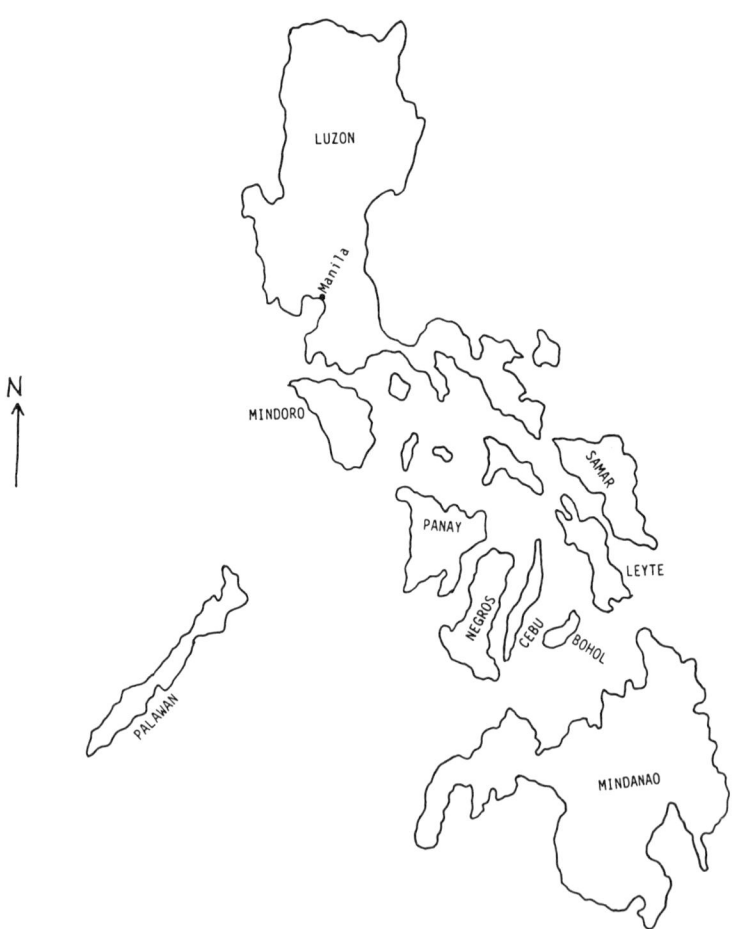

THE BATTLE OF MANILA 55

that raced back and forth between Hong Kong and Cavite carrying messages. The round-trip journey took nearly a week.

Manila was occupied by approximately thirteen thousand Spanish soldiers and was well defended by artillery. Dewey realized that, even if he bombarded the city to rubble, he could not claim possession until an army of occupation arrived from the United States. The commodore sent a cable from Hong Kong to John D. Long, secretary of the navy, stating that it would take from five to ten thousand troops to capture and hold Manila.

This new predicament placed the Department of the Army in a dilemma. The only troops available were volunteer organizations and whatever regiments could be spared from the frontier.

State volunteer units were quickly directed to proceed to San Francisco and await orders for shipment across the Pacific.

On May 12, Major General Wesley Merritt was ordered by President McKinley to organize the expeditionary force that was assembling on the west coast: "Go to the Philippines, cooperate with the Navy, defeat the Spanish armed forces there, and establish the sovereignty of the United States."

Meanwhile, without authority from the State Department, Pratt convinced Aguinaldo that, if he went back to the Philippines and stirred up another rebellion against the Spanish, the United States would grant independence to the Filipinos.

Pratt notified Dewey of his plan, and two weeks after the Battle of Manila Bay, Aguinaldo arrived at Cavite aboard the *McCulloch*. Although Aguinaldo later claimed that Dewey reiterated Spencer Pratt's promises, it is unlikely that the commodore was taken in by the clever revolutionary.

Aguinaldo immediately began issuing proclamations and assembling an army. On May 24, he proclaimed a dictatorial government with himself as the leader and promised the people a constitution similar to that of the United States.

The plight of the Spaniards in the Philippines was becoming desperate. Aguinaldo had aroused the natives throughout the island of Luzon, and Spanish garrisons throughout the archipelago were being attacked and overthrown. Within days, the rebels were at the gates of Manila. Dewey soon realized that, in permitting this revolutionary government to establish itself, he had created a Frankenstein.

The commander of the Spanish forces in Manila, Captain-General

Augustin Devila, frantically began secret meetings with the British consul in an effort to find a peaceful settlement of the crisis. Devila reported to Madrid: "We are besieged by land and sea. I shall try and resist to the last, but have no confidence in the result. Increasing numbers of volunteers and natives are deserting to the rebels."

The Spanish government, afraid that Devila was about to surrender the city, replaced him with General Firmin Jaudenes. However, Jaudenes was also aware that the situation was hopeless. In the meantime, the British consul had died, and the Belgian consul assumed the role as negotiator—this time with General Jaudenes.

The total number of American troops designated for service in the Philippines was arbitrarily set at 20,000, but moving the soldiers overseas became a problem. There was a shortage of ships on the Pacific coast, and many owners were reluctant to break up their commercial traffic and part with their vessels at any price. It was only after threats of seizure that enough ships were obtained to carry the army.

The first detachment of troops, under the command of General Thomas M. Anderson, sailed from San Francisco on May 23, 1898, aboard the steamers *City of Peking*, *City of Sidney*, and *Australia*. Among the embarking soldiers were men from the California and Oregon volunteers, and the Fourteenth Infantry Regiment.

The volunteers were dressed in regulation fatigues, while the Fourteenth Infantry wore their heavyweight field uniforms. Once again, the regulars were being sent to the tropics without summer clothing.

The people of San Francisco gave the soldiers a royal sendoff. Tugs and ferryboats followed the departing transports through the bay. A soldier, aboard the *Australia*, described the heart-stirring farewell: "As we pulled away from the dock, the throngs crowding the piers cheered and shouted words of encouragement. Adding to the commotion, regimental bands began to play 'Hail Columbia' and 'The Girl I Left Behind.'

"The troops, whose grave faces reflected their sober thoughts, yelled until their throats were sore—and then took feeble refuge in the frantic waving of flags. Women, jamming the wharves, choked down their sobs and shouted Godspeeds to loved ones—while tears, that would not hold back, ran unheeded down their furrowed cheeks.

"As we made our way out into the bay, dozens of 'good-bye' boats flocked about the transports. Tugboats, packed with well-wishers, blew their whistles incessantly and chugged close alongside our vessels. The tug passengers were almost able to shake hands with the soldiers who pressed against the guard-rails of the troopships. One innovative volunteer thrust his Springfield down to a teary-eyed young lady. She grabbed the end of the rifle barrel—bridging the gap between them.

"The excitement reached its peak when a large side-wheeler, flying the Red Cross flag, drew near the *Australia*. One of the ladies removed the badge from her sleeve and tossed it to the deck of the transport. A wild scramble for the souvenir resulted. Then dozens of other women removed the emblem from their uniforms and threw them to the troops—along with flowers, oranges, and box lunches.

"As land gradually disappeared in the twilight, the *City of Peking* showed off our starboard bow—her glimmering lights dancing above the water as she bowed to the shouldering swells. Off the port quarter, the lights of the *Sidney* picked up our escort, the U.S.S. *Charleston*, leading us into the unknown."

On June 14, a second group of soldiers left the west coast aboard the transports *China*, *Colon*, and *Zealandia*. This brigade was under the command of General Francis V. Greene, and included Colorado, Nebraska, and Pennsylvania volunteer units, plus batteries of the Utah Artillery. The regular army contingent was comprised of the Eighteenth and Twenty-third Infantry Regiments.

General Greene recalled the voyage: "We were a stately procession sailing across the calm, deserted Pacific—day after day—not seeing another ship, or land, or sign of life.

"Gunnery practice, both with rifles and artillery, was carried out at frequent intervals. The *China*, being the fastest vessel, would race ahead in the early morning, place a target, allow the troopships to fire at it as they passed, then pick up the target and rejoin the flotilla before dark. This was accomplished without diminishing the speed of the slowest ship."

The third convoy to the Philippines was under the command of General Arthur MacArthur and sailed from San Francisco on June 26. The four thousand troops making the voyage included the Wyoming, Idaho, and Minnesota volunteers—along with the Third Regular Artillery. General Merritt and his staff followed aboard the *Newport*.

A headquarters officer recounted the departure: "During the early morning hours, masses of people began to assemble near the regimental camps. Each soldier was handed a parcel containing food and other necessities—including the ominous abdominal bandage.

"About eleven o'clock, the bugles sounded and the men lined up in formation for the five mile hike to the waterfront. The crowds shouted and cheered as the troops paraded by. Relatives of some of the boys marched with them.

"It was a long hot tramp over cobblestones, but the Red Cross girls continually thrust glasses of cold water into the sweating hands of the thirsty soldiers.

"Once aboard their respective transports, the troops were given a tremendous ovation by the throngs of people who swarmed on and around the wharves. Hundreds of oranges were thrown by the crowd and caught by the appreciative men as their ships crept away from the docks."

The three-convoy military force bound for the Philippines was designated the Eighth Army Corps. General Elwell Otis was placed in command of the corps, and General Merritt was named head of the newly created Department of the Pacific.

While the American expedition was still on the high seas, Aguinaldo's rebels won a series of victories over the Spanish—capturing Cavite Province, Laguna, and other important districts.

Near the end of June, the Filipinos officially proclaimed a provisional government, and a declaration of independence was read renouncing Spanish authority. The Insurgents elected Aguinaldo as president and Daniel Perindo as vice-president. A cabinet, legislative body, and supreme court were formed.

In anticipation of a rebel attack on Manila, the Spaniards had constructed a formidable line of trenches and blockhouses that stretched in a semicircle about five miles from the city.

Meanwhile, the Insurgents barricaded every road leading into the capital and dug a series of rifle pits around the town. Manila was not only blockaded on the land side, but Dewey's fleet controlled the bay and harbor.

The continued success of Emilio Aguinaldo, and the possibility that he might attempt to attack and capture Manila before American troops arrived, began to cause grave concern in Washington.

However, the newly appointed Admiral Dewey was positive that the Spanish garrison would never surrender to the Insurgents—they would burn the city and die in the flames first. For this reason, Dewey calculated, the Spaniards would take the lesser of the two evils and capitulate to the United States.

The admiral knew he was sitting on a powder keg with a short fuse. The only thing needed was a lighted match to blow the revolution sky high and out of control. Dewey decided to let Aguinaldo continue with his operations, but kept the fleet on alert—ready to interfere if the Insurgent leader became too reckless.

General Anderson and the first group of American troops arrived at Manila Bay on July 1. They disembarked and camped on the grounds of the navy yard.

Anderson's aide described the first few days in the Philippines: "The arsenal and navy yard, with barracks and buildings for officers, occupy a half-mile of Cavite Point. The wrecks of three Spanish ships can be seen awash. But at low tide they are exposed enough to show the damage done by American naval shells. It gave one a curious sensation of pride, mixed with sympathy, to see the pitiable spectacle that the sunken Spanish ships presented.

"The tip of Point Cavite is occupied by an old fort. At one time, on top of its heavy stone parapets, stood several six- and eight-inch smooth bore cannons. They had been lugged away by the Insurgents' and dragged to their trenches near Malate.

"Behind the fort are machine-shops and storehouses. All kinds of work was going on, and complete facilities had been set up for almost any sort of maritime repairs.

"The Insurgents—dressed in striped blue cotton uniforms and straw hats—were permitted to work in the shops. The rebels made the most of their opportunity. They ripped the guns from sunken Spanish ships, and made breech locks to replace those thrown overboard by the Spaniards. Within a few days, the defenders of Manila were looking down the barrels of their own cannons.

"In one small hut near the navy yard, a beehive of Insurgents were busy cleaning and reloading cartridge shells. Nothing was wasted—the rebels managed to make everything serve their purpose.

"Facing Fort Felipe, on the Bakor Bay side of the point, was the house of the former Spanish commandant of the yard. This dwelling was taken over by the Fourteenth Infantry officers. General Anderson occupied the adjutant's house for brigade headquarters.

"The California volunteers were barracked behind San Felipe. There was also a separate building for the hospital, and another for the regimental bands. The Oregon soldiers were bivouacked outside the navy yard gate—next to a large field.

Map 4.2
American, Spanish and Insurgent Positions South of Manila, July 30, 1898

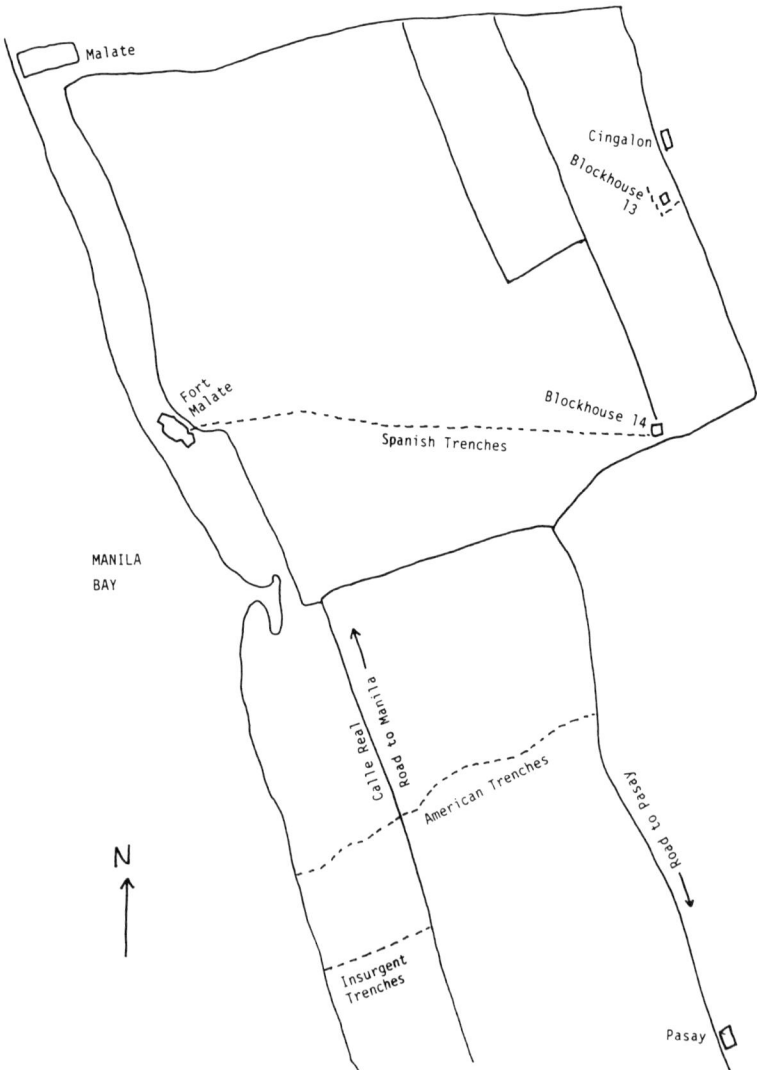

"On the other side of the clearing stretched the town of Old Cavite—with its vile-smelling, narrow streets. Only the top floors of the two-story dwellings were used for living quarters. The ground level spaces were taken up with shops and storerooms.

"Evidently nobody in the village ever heard of street cleaning. The roadways are not even guttered, and are littered with sewage and garbage. Whenever it rains, water stands a few feet deep in the first floor rooms. We not only boiled our water, but filtered it as well."

The Insurgents were in force in Old Cavite. The magnificent mansions, once the homes of wealthy Spaniards, were now the quarters for the rebel army. Aguinaldo used one large house for his residence. Another building, and its elegant grounds, served as a prison for two thousand captured Spanish soldiers.

Soon after his troops landed, General Anderson notified Aguinaldo that the entire Cavite Peninsula would be needed for additional American troops that were due to arrive. The rebel leader protested, but finally moved his men to Bakor—directly across the bay from Cavite.

Anderson realized that there might be future problems with the rebel chieftain, and notified Aguinaldo that the United States recognized his military leadership, but not his civil authority—and also that no other nation had done so.

Aguinaldo was furious. He considered Anderson's remarks a violation of the promises made by both Pratt and Dewey—and had expected the United States would be the first to recognize Philippine independence.

Emilio Aguinaldo was a prolific writer of letters and proclamations. He wrote a bitter letter to Rouseville Wildman, the American consul in Hong Kong. Wildman reassured the Insurgent leader that the United States was not fighting the Spanish War "for the love of conquest or the hope of gain," and that the Filipinos would be treated with honor and justice by the American government.

When this news reached the State Department, Wildman was immediately censured: "Your action disapproved and you are forbidden to make pledges or discuss policy."

General Greene's convoy steamed into Manila Bay on July 15. The morning after his arrival, Anderson and Greene scouted the mainland for a place to land troops. A site was picked out about a mile below the Insurgent lines. Greene wrote in his report: "We selected a flat field about four feet above flood tide. It was a mile and a half long by a quarter-mile wide, and enclosed on three sides by dense thickets of bamboo and rice swamps. The fourth side was a sandy beach.

"The area was large enough to accommodate about eight thousand men. To the north, the field was just out of range of Spanish musket fire—but not enemy field artillery. Preparations for disembarking the soldiers were begun the following morning."

General Anderson divided the regiments into two brigades. The first unit was comprised of California and Oregon volunteers—the Twenty-third and Fourteenth Infantries—and Battery A of the Utah Artillery.

The second brigade, under the command of General Greene, included the Colorado, Nebraska, and Pennsylvania volunteers—along with the Eighteenth Infantry Regiment and Battery B of the Utah Artillery.

Greene's brigade was picked to land on the beach and establish a campsite near the Insurgent lines. However, logistical problems were immediately encountered during the amphibious operation. Not a single horse or wagon had been brought from the United States to carry men and supplies.

General Anderson assumed that the Filipino rebels were subordinate allies, and would provide goods and services required by the American Army. Anderson sent a message to Aguinaldo stating that he wished to hire carts, horses, and native labor to help transport the American soldiers and their equipment inland from the beach.

Aguinaldo refused the request and informed Anderson that wagons were not available. It was soon discovered that the Insurgent commander had made a list of all carts in the district and informed the owners that they were not to engage in any service for the Americans without his permission. The natives removed the wheels from their wagons and hid them. Anderson was irritated by Aguinaldo's refusal to cooperate, but decided to go ahead with the planned operation.

Since the landing site was within range of Spanish artillery, it was thought best not to bring the transports too near the shore. A dozen flat-bottom boats and a couple of small tugs had been captured by Admiral Dewey—and these were utilized to ferry the troops to the beach.

General Greene described the amphibious landing: "Each barge was loaded to capacity with men and supplies. During flood tide, a string of three or four barges were towed by each tugboat to the beach. The men jumped into the water and waded ashore. When the tide receded, they returned and unloaded their supplies. Everything was hauled to the campsite on the backs of the soldiers."

THE BATTLE OF MANILA 63

The first group of men splashed ashore after dark, but the rest of the troops reached the beach in broad daylight. Surprisingly, the Spaniards did not open fire or interfere in any way. The entire 4,000-man brigade was landed without mishap.

General Anderson remained at Cavite with 2,000 reserves pending the arrival of Merritt and MacArthur.

The *Newport* steamed into Manila Bay on July 25, and General Merritt assumed command of all expeditionary forces in the Philippines. When General MacArthur's convoy arrived a few days later, Merritt felt that his corps was now strong enough to attack Manila successfully. The troops were organized into a division under General Anderson and consisted of two brigades. General MacArthur was placed in command of the First Brigade, and General Greene headed the Second Brigade.

A staff conference was called and a strategy formulated. However, Aguinaldo was not notified of the American plans. General Merritt wrote: "As Aguinaldo did not visit me on my arrival, nor offer his services as a subordinate military leader, and as my instructions from the President fully contemplated the occupation of the islands by American land forces, and stated that 'the powers of the military occupant are absolute and supreme,' I did not consider it wise to hold any direct communication with the Insurgent leader until I should be in possession of the city of Manila."

However, Merritt had one delicate problem to solve. Insurgent entrenchments completely surrounded the city. There was no way for the corps to advance on Manila without running over the rebel trenches. It was necessary that a section of the Insurgent rifle pits be turned over to American troops.

The Insurgent line in front of the Eighth Army Corps encampment (now named Camp Dewey) was commanded by General Noriel. Merritt asked General Anderson to approach Noriel with a request that the Filipinos move over and permit American forces to occupy trenches in front of Camp Dewey, in order that field artillery could be moved up and trained on Spanish positions.

General Noriel agreed to take the matter up with his superiors. Aguinaldo reluctantly gave permission—while at the same time stating that he was still relying on the assurances he had been given concerning Philippine independence.

The following morning, one battalion each from the Colorado volunteers and Eighteenth Infantry—along with a battery of Utah Artillery—occupied the Insurgent entrenchments closest to the beach.

It was not long, however, before General Greene became cognizant of the fact that the rebel trenches were too shallow and not well located. General Merritt was immediately notified of the difficulty and ordered another trench constructed about 125 yards closer to the Spanish lines. The American soldiers shoveled day and night—most of the time in pouring rain. Bamboo poles were used to keep the dugout walls from collapsing. By the evening of July 29, the sandbagged rifle pits extended three hundred yards inland—from the shore to the Pasay road.

From the time that the Spanish-American conflict began, President McKinley had been the object of a tug of war between the Imperialists and Anti-Imperialists factions in the United States. The battle cry "Manifest Destiny" became the slogan of the Imperialists from coast to coast. Carl Schurz, a former senator from Missouri, defined the precept: "The new 'Manifest Destiny' means not merely the incorporation by the United States of territory contiguous to its borders—but also the acquisition of such territory, far and near, as may be useful in enlarging our commercial advantages, and in securing, for our Navy, facilities desirable for the operations of a great naval power."

As the war wound down to a close, McKinley made up his mind which course the country was to take: "When the war is over we must keep what we want."

After General Toral surrendered at Santiago, the Spanish government sued for peace—and on July 30, 1898, President McKinley stated his terms: "Spain must get out of Cuba, Puerto Rico, and Guam—plus turn over the city, bay, and harbor of Manila to occupation by United States forces."

The dramatic news fell on the Filipino Insurgents like a brick wall—they had been sold down the river. Aguinaldo immediately had his new government ratify the Proclamation of Independence, and sent messages to all foreign officials asking for recognition.

Aguinaldo also demanded that the rebel army be a part of any force liberating Manila: "It is unthinkable that after so many years of revolutionary struggle, victory should be taken out of our hands at the last moment by the United States Army."

However, when General Merritt arrived at Cavite, he already had his orders from the president: "There must be no joint occupation of Manila with the Insurgents. Use any means in your judgment necessary to this end. The rebels must recognize the military occupation and authority of the United States."

President McKinley's decision to occupy the Philippine Islands made it imperative to keep Aguinaldo and his soldiers out of the capital city. The United States would be seriously embarrassed if the Insurgents overthrew the Spanish government and established one of their own at Manila. McKinley would have found it difficult to justify further possession of the archipelago.

There was also the fear that native uprisings might result in wholesale massacres of foreign nationals—which would involve the United States in dangerous complications with other governments.

On the evening of August 1, four companies of Pennsylvania volunteers and the Third Artillery were ordered into the new American trenches. At ten o'clock, heavy firing erupted all along the Spanish front. The enemy shelling was extremely accurate. A perfect hailstorm of bullets and artillery pounded the American positions. General Greene wrote in his report concerning the night action: "Pickets, who had been posted on our right flank, came back and announced that the Spanish infantry was attempting to swing around behind our positions. My trenches did not extend east of the Pasay road, and the ground to the right was only protected by small clusters of bamboo, shrubs, and tall grass."

The Spaniards continued their furious attack and advanced far enough to have Greene's troops in a crossfire. The Pennsylvania soldiers became excited and began shooting wildly.

Captain O'Hara, commanding the Third Artillery, had been keeping track of American firing and knew that the men in the trenches would soon be out of ammunition. Without waiting for orders, he had his gun crews grab their rifles and assemble as infantrymen.

O'Hara took an orderly and bugler with him, and headed for the Pasay road. He instructed Captain Hobbs to follow with the troops when the bugle sounded.

As Captain O'Hara reached the roadway, he met a courier who told him that the Americans were taking a beating. The captain ordered the bugler to sound charge. O'Hara then took off running in the direction of the besieged rifle pits—shouting to the Pennsylvania boys that reinforcements were on the way.

At the sound of the bugle call, Hobbs led his men in double column. They raced across the clearing between the Insurgent trenches and the American breastworks. Spanish guns swept the ground—making the field a death trap.

Lieutenant Krayenbuhl's platoon was in the lead and ran headlong into a group of advancing Spaniards. The surprised artillerymen began shooting indiscriminately. Krayenbuhl drew his revolver and threatened to shoot the first man who fired without orders. The soldiers quickly calmed down and deployed as skirmishers. Accurate volleys soon stopped the enemy advance.

Captain Hobbs was wounded in the leg, but kept on moving. The Spaniards filled the air with bullets. Lieutenant Kessler's platoon reached the American trenches only moments before the Pennsylvania detachment ran out of ammunition. Hobbs climbed painfully to the crest of the earthworks and directed the fire of his men.

Meanwhile, the courier had reached General Greene's headquarters and reported that the battle was lost. Greene immediately called up his reserves. A battalion of California volunteers was sent racing across the open field through a barrage of bullets and shells. However, in the darkness they mistakenly jumped into the Insurgent rifle pits. The Californians fired three volleys at their own lines before they discovered the error and continued their dash to the American entrenchments.

Private J. F. Finley hauled an ammunition cart across the deadly clearing to the trenches. On his return trip, he picked up two wounded men and delivered them to the field hospital. Finley then went back for another wagon load of wounded soldiers. The battle raged for nearly five savage hours before the Spanish attack was repulsed.

When the American brigades sailed from San Francisco, General Anderson had only been able to obtain enough ammunition to supply each soldier with 400 rounds. (When the Manila garrison finally surrendered, the Spaniards still had 700 rounds per man.)

After the first night of combat, the shortage of ammunition became critical. General Merritt issued strict conservation orders. General Greene stated: "My instructions were not only to remain on the defensive, but not even answer the enemy's fire. It was not easy to carry out this directive—for nothing is more trying for soldiers than to sit still under fire, and in the darkness it was very difficult to see if the Spaniards were advancing."

The rainy season had also begun to take its toll. A typhoon blew in from the South China Sea making it virtually impossible for many of the men aboard MacArthur's ships to disembark, as well as for most of the supplies to be unloaded. An attempt was made to bring provisions and ammunition to the beach, but the barges were swamped in the stormy surf.

During the next six nights, the Spanish launched three more assaults against the American positions, but General Merritt stuck to his policy of no return fire. A quick inventory had revealed that the Eighth Army Corps had only enough ammunition for a single day of heavy combat.

Meanwhile negotiations continued between General Jaudenes and the Belgian consul. Jaudenes finally agreed to surrender if General Merritt would bar the Insurgents from entering Manila, and if Admiral Dewey's fleet would not shell the city. In return, the Spanish promised not to use their large caliber siege guns against the Americans.

However, there was still one pressing problem confronting General Jaudenes—how to surrender and "save face" at the same time. Madrid would hold him directly responsible if he capitulated without a fight.

Therefore, a series of staged events began to take place. A battle was arranged—choreographed by the Belgian consul, and starring George Dewey, Wesley Merritt, and Firmin Jaudenes. The Spanish commander stated that, once his outer perimeter of defenses was captured, he would raise a white flag at a southwest point of the walled city.

On August 7, 1898, the plan was put into operation. General Merritt and Admiral Dewey sent a joint message to General Jaudenes demanding surrender of the Spanish Manila garrison: "We have the honor to notify your excellency that operations by the land and naval forces of the United States against the defenses of Manila may begin at any time after forty-eight hours from your receipt of this communication. This notice is given to afford you an opportunity to remove all noncombatants from the city."

Jaudenes replied, thanking the Americans for their "humane sentiments," but also stating: "The Council of Defense declared that your request cannot be granted. However, I would consult my government if your excellencies will grant the time necessary for this communication by way of Hong Kong."

Merritt's answer was short and curt: "In reply, we respectfully inform your excellency that we decline to grant the time requested."

The rainy season had already started, and it was apparent to General Merritt that action had to be taken at once to capture the city and relieve the troops in the trenches from the weather, sickness, and disease. Merritt wrote: "It was agreed, between Admiral Dewey and myself, that an attempt be made to carry the extreme right of the Spanish line of entrenchments—while the enemy's flank on the bay was entirely open to naval gunfire."

By August 10, General MacArthur's troops had been transferred ashore, and the Fourteenth and Twenty-third Regiments, held in reserve at Cavite, were also ferried across to Camp Dewey.

A joint naval and land assault on the Spanish positions was planned for the early morning of August 13. General Merritt stated: "It was not my intention to press the attack along the beach until the navy had made breaches in the enemy works at Fort Malate. This could not be done by the army alone due to our lack of siege guns."

To the front of the American division stretched a mile of Spanish trenches—anchored on the west side at Fort Malate, and on the east by a masonry and wood blockhouse—a large number 14 emblazoned on its side.

Seven battalions of Greene's Second Brigade were stationed from the bay to the Calle Real—while eight battalions of MacArthur's First Brigade occupied trenches from the roadway to the woods and swamps on the right of the American line.

General MacArthur was also instructed to station detachments of troops in all captured rifle pits—and "permit no armed bodies, other than American soldiers, to cross the trenches in the direction of Manila." The Insurgent forces of Emilio Aguinaldo were to be kept out of the city.

In the meantime, negotiations for an end to the conflict were progressing rapidly. The Queen Regent of Spain authorized the French Ambassador in Washington to sign a peace agreement ending hostilities between her country and the United States. That same day, a cable was sent to General Merritt by way of Hong Kong: "The President directs that all military operations against the enemy be suspended. Peace negotiations are nearing completion—a protocol just having been signed by representatives of the two countries. You will inform the commander of Spanish forces in the Philippines of these instructions. Further orders will follow. Acknowledge receipt."

(The Spanish-American War lasted 113 days, but would not officially end until the Treaty of Paris on December 10, 1898. However, as one historian stated: "Had we been pitted against any power other than Spain, the result would have been a catastrophe.")

Meanwhile, as the *McCulloch* was pounding at full speed across the South China Sea with news that the war had ended, the Eighth Army Corps launched its attack. (The dispatch boat did not arrive at Cavite until August 16.)

One of the artillery units attached to General MacArthur's command, and stationed on the far right of the American line, was the Astor Battery. At the beginning of the war, Colonel John Jacob Astor offered to equip an artillery outfit at his own expense. The secretary of war, Russell Alger, suggested a mountain battery similar to the type used by the English.

The Astor Battery was composed of about one hundred men, and six twelve-pound rapid fire Hotchkiss guns. Lieutenant March of the Fifth Artillery was appointed commanding officer. The soldiers were also armed with revolvers and sabers.

Each member of the detachment was hand-picked from his past service record. The result was a collection of soldiers who had seen military service in all parts of the world. A number of college volunteers were also included. One of the troopers, J. W. Watterson of Boston, had been decorated twice while serving in the British Army.

Regular light artillery pieces were permanently attached to carriages, and their movements limited to passable roads and open plains. Mountain batteries, however, were portable. Four pack mules were needed to transport each artillery piece. One mule carried the tube, another the carriage, and the other two hauled the ammunition. The guns and carriages were constructed so that they could be quickly disassembled and strapped on the backs of the animals. The mules were able to climb hills and travel over rugged terrain—impossible for ordinary artillery.

Captain T. Bentley Mott described the opening hours of the assault on Manila: "On the morning of August 13, the regiments were awakened at four o'clock. After breakfast we began our march to the front. Everybody was happy to leave soggy Camp Dewey after spending weeks in the rain and mud. But, as luck would have it, within a few minutes it began to rain again. The roadway became a muddy trough. It poured for two hours, and carrying orders along the line meant wading through muddy water up to the knees.

"By the time the troops were in position, the rain ceased and the air cleared. Our ships could be seen moving up the bay. About ten o'clock, a salvo from the *Olympia* crashed into Fort Malate. That was General Greene's signal for artillery to commence firing. The field guns methodically chewed off the crest of the fort—only one volley was fired in return.

"A battalion of Colorado volunteers was ordered forward across the swampy ground between the shore and the Calle Real. A second battalion followed in support. Two other companies were sent up the beach toward Malate. Both lines moved rapidly—the column on the right firing volleys at the Spanish trenches to cover the men moving north along the shoreline.

"The Malate fortifications were rushed and quickly captured. Lieutenant Colonel McCoy climbed the fort's flagpole and ripped off the Spanish ensign. A moment later, the Stars and Stripes floated from the staff—amid rousing cheers from the army and the fleet."

In a letter to his brother, Private Watterson chronicled the role that the Astor Battery played in the attack: "We left Camp Dewey on the evening of August 12 for the trenches. A violent thunderstorm was raging. The rain was coming down hard and fast. The water and mud were too deep for the mules. We used ropes and sleds to drag our guns, shells, shovels, axes, and hardtack. The distance, more than four miles, was over the worst ground I have ever wallowed through. It was impossible to see more than two yards ahead, and we often fell into holes up to our shoulders. The guns were completely covered by water. However, we held on to the drag ropes and pulled them out of the ditches. We were exhausted by the time we arrived at the breastworks, and slept in a banana patch, in the mud and rain, until five o'clock the next morning.

"We had just finished our coffee, when an Insurgent force to our right began firing. The Spaniards answered with a fierce cannonade. We quickly moved out—hacking a path through a bamboo thicket, and brought our guns out two hundred yards from the Spanish blockhouse 14.

"A continuous barrage of enemy shells and bullets whistled over our heads—cutting off the branches of trees. The Mauser bullets seemed to explode whenever they hit a bamboo pole—but I believe the noise ,was caused by the release of trapped air inside the bamboo stalk.

"Due to the narrow space (the Insurgents had crowded us on the right), only three of our guns could be brought into position. We immediately opened fire on the fort, and planted shell after shell into the blockhouse. However, the Spaniards had our range calibrated to the yard. Their first salvo exploded a few feet from my head. A flying splinter knocked the hat over my eyes, but I did not get a scratch. Another piece of the same shell tore away a spoke from one of the gun carriages—sliced off the barrel of Private Dunn's revolver—plowed through his canteen—and then ripped away eight inches of his right thigh muscle.

"By this time our shells had set fire to the blockhouse, and the enemy's ammunition started to explode. The Spaniards began to rush from the fort—firing at us as they ran. We dragged two of our guns over the breastworks and pursued the fleeing soldiers. A few of our men had cold feet and were left behind.

"When we reached the blockhouse, it was deserted. But the scene resembled a Fourth of July celebration—with all the ammunition going off in tremendous explosions. We climbed the vacated enemy trenches and managed, with great difficulty, to haul our guns over the top. We chased the Spaniards to the nearby village of Cingalon where they had another blockhouse near a small church.

"In the meantime, Dewey's fleet had been shelling the Spanish positions and chasing the enemy inland in our direction. We began firing at the approaching Spaniards, but our unit was vastly outnumbered. We only had one Minnesota company to the rear as support.

"Our guns soon became hot and choked with mud and sand. When the Spanish detachment in the blockhouse noticed that we were having trouble, they rushed our position. General MacArthur spotted the emergency and shouted for a captain and 'men of nerve' to take that fort. The infantry did not move. There was a momentary pause. Then the men of the Astor Battery drew their revolvers and dashed forward—firing and shouting like Comanche Indians. The Spaniards turned around and hurried frantically back to the blockhouse.

"While we attempted to return to our guns, the Spaniards inside the fort cut loose with a devastating Mauser barrage. We dashed for shelter behind a battered wood fence. The few boards where I was partly hidden were hit forty times by bullets just above my head. Several of us managed to crawl under a native hut and began shooting.

"We were caught between two fires. The Spanish were blasting us from the front, and the Minnesota boys were firing from behind. Sergeant Sillman was wounded in the leg. First Sergeant Holmes was a few feet from me. As he tried to bandage Sillman's leg, Holmes was struck in the head—the bullet tearing away five inches of his skull.

"Sergeant Crimmins was killed trying to get to his gun. About eight more men were wounded. One bullet hit my canteen and another ripped my shirt. We finally managed to reach our guns and soon forced the Spaniards from their position.

"General MacArthur personally thanked us, and the infantry gave the Astor Battery a rousing cheer. It is seldom in history that a fortress is charged by men with only pistols as weapons. We were called 'tin soldiers' at San Francisco, but are looked upon as heroes here."

With the enemy flanked on both sides, the Eighteenth Infantry and Third Artillery were ordered to attack the Spanish trenches at the center of the line. The assault was made across muddy ground and in the face of determined resistance.

MacArthur's brigade swung to the right of the Third Artillery and cleared the woods of enemy soldiers. The Twenty-third Infantry and Minnesota volunteers were then sent forward to support the frontal attack.

When the Colorado regiment reached the outskirts of Manila, a white flag was noticed flying from the western bastion of the city walls.

General Merritt, escorted by an Oregon company, entered Manila, and within a short time, the Stars and Stripes were floating over the Governor-General's Palace. The city was placed under martial law, and guards were stationed at the homes of foreign nationals to prevent looting.

The night before the attack, Merritt notified Aguinaldo that Insurgent soldiers must not enter Manila in the event that the city was captured by American forces. Aguinaldo was bitter. His men had done most of the fighting and dying—and now they were denied the honor as liberators of their own country.

Early on the morning of the 13th, the rebels began their own assault on the Spanish positions. They then followed behind General Anderson's advancing brigades, and occupied several Manila suburbs and some of the Spanish entrenchments.

The following day, General Merritt issued a proclamation establishing a "Government of Military Occupation" of the Philippines. The Insurgents were ordered to withdraw from the trenches they had captured and to remain outside the city.

General Anderson was given the thankless job of trying to pacify Aguinaldo—but the situation was rapidly getting out of hand. The rebels controlled the waterworks and cut off Manila's water supply. Anderson was forced to make certain concessions in order to have the water turned on again.

On August 21, the steamer *Arizona* arrived at Cavite with General Elwell Otis and 1,200 additional troops. The strength of the American garrison in Manila was now 14,000 men. A week later, General Merritt left for the Spanish-American Peace Conference in Paris. Otis assumed the duties as commander of all United States military forces in the Philippines.

The final disposition of the islands was now contingent upon the peace negotiations, but when the Spanish and American delegations met in October, no Filipinos were present.

The signing of the Treaty of Paris on December 10, 1898, ceded the Philippine Islands to the United States for 20 million dollars. The American Imperialists were now able to claim that the United States had purchased the islands as well as having won them in battle. (The treaty was ratified by the U.S. Senate in February 1899.)

Meanwhile, Emilio Aguinaldo was still boiling over the way he had been manipulated by the Americans. On September 9, 1898, he pulled back his troops and retreated with his staff to Malolos—about twenty-five miles north of Manila—where he established his own Philippine Republic.

The Insurgent leader immediately proceeded to levy taxes, issue proclamations, and impose travel restrictions on Americans. Through gun dealers, Aguinaldo was able to purchase ten thousand Mauser and Remington rifles—more than 3 million rounds of ammunition—and several artillery pieces. He was soon ready to march on Manila with twenty-thousand armed, angry men. The Philippine Islands were about to explode.

Chapter Five

REVOLT IN THE PHILIPPINES

During the Twenty-second Regiment's four months at Fort Crook, Captain Jacob Kreps had been whipping his fledgling company into shape. He remembered the first rookie assigned to his command: "Private Henry W. Johnson was a smooth-faced, light-haired boy from the farming district of Illinois. He was quiet and retiring in his manner—and assuredly without the appearance of a soldier. He seemed out of place in a regiment that would soon be leaving for the Philippines—destined to face dangers beyond the imagination. I often wondered why Johnson enlisted in the army. Was it patriotism, or the desire to escape from the contracted circle of his daily life, that caused him to take this step?"

On January 27, 1899, the Twenty-second Infantry received orders to proceed to California by rail. The troops were issued gray campaign hats and waterproof pith helmets—with a hood attached that covered the back of the neck and shoulders. Each man received a pair of heavy campaign trousers—two pair of army boots and leggings—two blue woolen shirts—and a pair of gauntlet-type buckskin gloves.

The regiment arrived at San Francisco on the 31st, and boarded the steamers *Senator* and *Ohio*. Captain Kreps and Company M were packed in the cargo spaces of the *Senator*. Jacob Kreps wrote: "When we pulled away from the wharf, it seemed to many of the men that the ties that bound us so agreeably to life were being ruthlessly severed. The strains of the Presidio Band, sent in to speed us on our way, played 'The Girl

I Left Behind' in maddening cadence. It appeared a hollow mockery to those separated from wives, sweethearts, and babies—perhaps forever.

"A wave of miserable, helpless homesickness swept over me—and as the music of the band slowly faded, the sounds of the wind and sea took its place. The shores of our homeland soon disappeared from sight, and my sentimental feelings were outranked by the swaying and bouncing of our little transport—which began to cause a responsive discontent in my internal organs. The general instability of all things maritime, combined with the hot disagreeable odors from below decks, quickly drove all personal thoughts from my mind."

While the ships carrying the Twenty-second Infantry were steaming slowly across the Pacific, tensions between the American troops and the Filipinos continued to grow. The Insurgents surrounded Manila, and occupied most of the old Spanish blockhouses and trenches. These defenses completely enclosed the city in an irregular semicircle extending from the outskirts of Manila on the north to a couple of miles south of Malate.

The blockhouses were approximately a mile apart, and were numbered from north to south—one to fifteen. Four of the blockhouses—numbers 8, 10, 11, and 12—were within American lines on both sides of the Pasig River.

General Otis divided his corps into two divisions of two brigades each. The First Division was under the command of General Thomas Anderson and was stationed south of the Pasig River.

Anderson's First Brigade was headed by General Charles King, and comprised the California, Washington, Idaho, and Wyoming volunteers. They occupied a line from the river to blockhouse 12.

The Second Brigade was commanded by General Samuel Ovenshine, and included the Fourteenth Infantry, six troops of the Fourth Cavalry, and the North Dakota volunteers. Ovenshine's brigade patrolled the area from blockhouse 12 to Malate.

Anderson also had in reserve, two batteries of the Sixth Artillery, four guns of the Astor Battery, and one company of engineers acting as infantry.

The Second Division was commanded by General Arthur MacArthur and was bivouacked north of the Pasig River.

MacArthur's First Brigade, under General Harrison Gray Otis, extended from the bay north of Manila to a point four hundred yards

Map 5.1
Position of Nebraska Volunteer Regiment and Insurgent Blockhouses, February 2, 1899

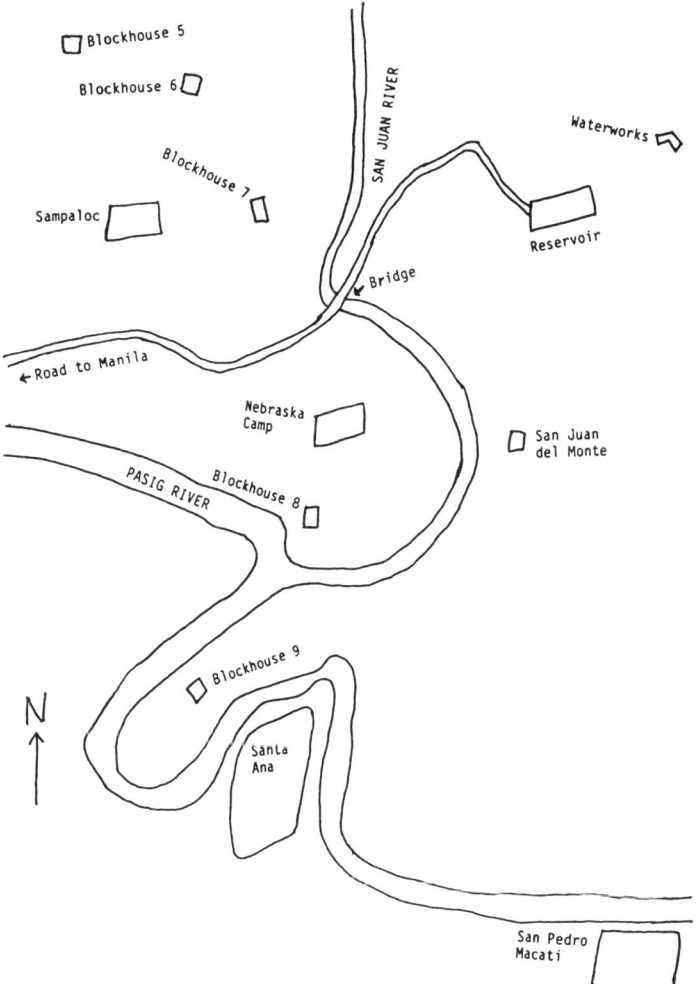

southwest of blockhouse 4. This brigade consisted of troops from the Kansas, Montana, and Pennsylvania volunteers—along with the Third Artillery.

The Second Brigade, headed by General Irving Hale, patrolled the front from blockhouses 4 to 8—near the junction of the Pasig and San Juan Rivers. Hale's soldiers included the South Dakota, Colorado, and Nebraska volunteers.

The Dakota troops were stationed at San Miguel near blockhouse 5. The Colorado detachment, at Sampoloc, defended against number 6—whereas the Nebraska lines stretched to Santa Mesa, opposite blockhouses 7 and 8—the extreme point inland occupied by American forces.

During the month of January 1899, the two armies faced one another, each waiting for the other to provoke an attack. Minor incidents were reported to General MacArthur, but an exchange of letters between the two parties settled the disputes.

On February 2, MacArthur sent a complaint to the Insurgent colonel whose troops faced the Nebraska front: "The line between your territory and mine has long been established and well understood. However, an armed patrol from your command now occupies the village in front of blockhouse 7 at a point considerably more than a hundred yards on my side of the line. This party must be withdrawn at once. From this date, if the line is crossed by your men, with arms in their hands, they will be regarded as subject to such action as I may deem necessary."

The Insurgent officer replied that he would issue orders to have his troops retire immediately, but at 8:30 on the evening of February 4, the simmering pot finally boiled over.

A Filipino patrol was spotted as it crossed the American front near blockhouse 7. Private Willie Grayson challenged the Insurgents twice—but when they continued to advance, he fired his rifle. The rebels dashed into the blockhouse and began shooting at the Nebraska positions. Other Filipino units took up the attack, and the Nebraskans retaliated. A regimental officer wrote: "The volunteers responded with spirit—their Springfields flashing in a half-moon around our perimeter. The enemy Mausers showed no flash to reveal their location."

Sporadic firing continued at intervals until about four o'clock the next morning. At that time, a large group of Insurgents shouting "Viva la Republica" attempted to rush the San Juan Bridge leading to the waterworks. A Nebraska company met the rebels at the crossing and drove them back three times before the enemy withdrew.

Upon hearing that his troops were under attack by American forces, Aguinaldo immediately issued a declaration of war against the United States: "About nine o'clock on the evening of February 4, American soldiers, without prior notification or any just motive, attacked our camp at San Juan del Monte, and our forces garrisoning a blockhouse around the outskirts of Manila.

"It is my duty to maintain the integrity of our national honor, and that of the army so unjustly attacked by those, who posing as our friends and liberators, attempt to dominate us in place of the Spaniards.

"Summoned by this unexpected provocation—urged by the duties imposed upon me by honor and patriotism—and for the defense of the nation entrusted to me, I hereby order and command: Peace and friendly relations between the Philippine Republic and the American army of occupation are broken—and the latter will be treated as enemies with the limits prescribed by the laws of war. American soldiers who may be captured by the Philippine forces will be treated as prisoners of war."

Soon after daybreak, Lieutenant Webb of Battery A, Utah Artillery, opened fire on blockhouse 5 and its earthworks. At 8:30, Colonel McCoy and three Colorado companies rushed the fortress and surrounding trenches. Three other companies, commanded by Lieutenant Colonel Moses, captured the rebel positions between blockhouses 5 and 6.

Colonel Stotsenberg, with two Nebraska companies, captured blockhouses 6 and 7. They then stormed across the San Juan bridge—followed by two artillery detachments.

The Nebraskans met stiff resistance on the bridge. They were caught out in the open. The men crouched in pairs as they worked their way over the span amid a hail of Mauser bullets.

A Tennessee battalion immediately followed the Nebraska troops. They advanced in columns of four under steady enemy fire.

Colonel Frost's South Dakota regiment charged blockhouse 4 and then turned to help Stotsenberg's men who were pinned down by rebel forces on high ground.

On a hill to the Nebraska left was a small Chinese church and cemetery. Behind the cemetery was the La Loma Church. Both were occupied by the Insurgents, who poured a devastating Mauser barrage down on the Americans. The slope to the enemy position was not steep, but the Nebraskans were forced to fight their way across a mile of rugged country that was barricaded by barbed wire entanglements.

Map 5.2
Insurgent Blockhouses and La Loma Church Guarding the Approaches to Caloocan

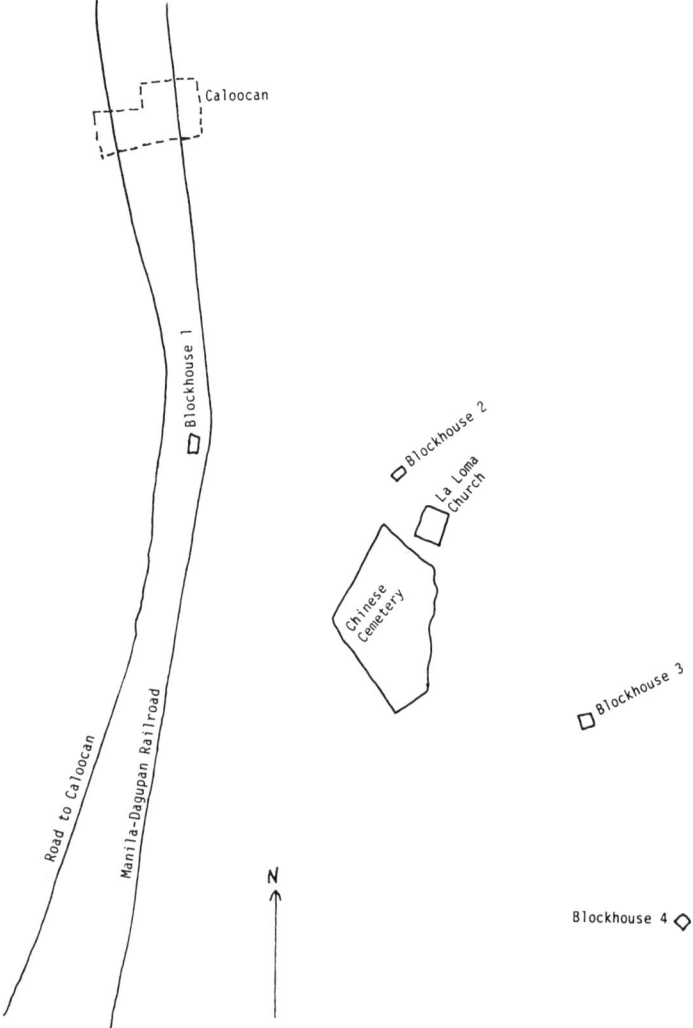

Meanwhile, General Harrison Otis and a brigade of Kansas, Montana, and Pennsylvania troops advanced under heavy fire toward the Chinese cemetery and the La Loma Church.

The Utah and Third Artillery batteries were called up to the front to blast the rebel stronghold. The Utah guns supported Stotsenberg's attack—ripping the barbed wire defenses as the Americans moved forward.

Captain O'Hara and two batteries of the Third Artillery hurried along the dikes separating the rice fields. O'Hara positioned his guns directly facing the front of the La Loma Church. After a few salvos, the Insurgents were chased out into the open, where they came under the killing fire of the infantry regiments. Very few of the Filipinos escaped the merciless attack of the American sharpshooters.

General Harrison Otis immediately entrenched his position. The Utah Artillery was stationed at the northeast corner of the churchyard, and the Pennsylvania and South Dakota volunteers covered the cemetery from the southeast.

At first it seemed that most of the action was taking place north of the Pasig River. However, General Anderson's brigades also had their hands full on the south bank.

At three o'clock on the morning of the 5th, the Insurgents attacked blockhouse 11—which was in the American zone. Anderson wrote in his report: "I directed General Ovenshine to commence an artillery barrage at daybreak on the enemy occupied blockhouse 14 and nearby woods. If successful, he was to sweep the rebels from his entire front—then reinforce General King's right. Both brigades would swing left to Santa Ana, trapping a large group of Insurgents between our army and the river."

The Sixth Artillery opened fire about seven o'clock, and a couple of hours later, Ovenshine ordered his troops to move out. Major Potter's battalion of Fourteenth Infantry attacked the woods to the right of blockhouse 14, while Captain John Murphy and his battalion charged the fort and its adjoining trenches.

Enemy resistance at the blockhouse was stubborn. The bastion was only four hundred yards away, but it might as well have been a couple of thousand.

Finally, after six hours of combat, Lieutenant Miles and his company battled their way into the rifle pits. Miles called for volunteers to rush the blockhouse. He chose eight men and charged the rebel position.

As the Americans burst into the fort, they met the Insurgents coming out. The Filipinos were no match for the regulars, and the blockhouse was captured. It had been a vicious engagement with heavy losses on both sides. The ground between the American and Insurgent lines was nicknamed "Bloody Lane."

After the victory at blockhouse 14, General Ovenshine's brigade swung left across an open field toward a bamboo grove being used by enemy snipers. The rebels were soon routed, and the brigade hurried on to Pasay.

When Ovenshine reached the city, he found it abandoned. He stationed a few companies in the town and marched with the rest of his command toward San Pedro Macati to link up with General King's brigade.

However, King had run into stiff enemy resistance. General Anderson ordered Colonel Smith of the California volunteers to assemble three of his companies along with four from the Wyoming regiment and support General King's advance on the city. King was directed to launch an attack on San Pedro Macati as soon as Smith had deployed his troops.

General King described the assault: "Upon my signal, the troops charged over a creek to our front. There were cheers and rattling volleys as the whole line advanced with a rush. The Insurgents fell back—fighting, however, with spirit. The rice fields ahead of us were intersected by irrigating ditches, and the Filipinos made a determined stand behind each of these defenses. The fields were soon dotted with dead and wounded. Sixty-five enemy bodies were found in one heap.

"Our men moved steadily forward until a raking fire was opened up on them from an earthwork at the neck of the bend of the Pasig River between Padacan and Santa Ana. The Idaho troops swung left and carried the breastworks with a bayonet charge—driving the Insurgents to the banks of the river."

Battery D of the Sixth Artillery, under Captain Dyers, and a Montana battery commanded by Captain Hawthorne, continually shelled the rebels as the American line advanced.

Colonel Smith's men broke through the Insurgent's left flank and charged into Santa Ana. The defenders put up a vigorous fight—battling from house to house, and setting each dwelling on fire as they retreated.

The Wyoming companies, on the right of Smith's line, were unable to keep up with the advance, and the enemy forces escaped to San Pedro Macati where they regrouped to defend the city. Barricades were hurriedly constructed around the town, and the Insurgents also occupied a church and the monastery of Guadalupe.

General King's brigade fought its way to the outskirts of San Pedro Macati, but American attacks against the city were repeatedly beaten back. The battle was a stand-off until a company of engineers managed to force their way into the town from the rear.

King's brigade launched another assault—this time bursting through the enemy's outer defenses and into the city. The Washington, Idaho, and Wyoming troops smashed their way along the riverfront and linked up with the engineers.

The Insurgents were trapped, but once again the battle raged from one burning building to another. Fire and smoke encircled the city like a gigantic bonfire.

By the late afternoon of February 5, the First Division had extended its lines from Pasay to the Pasig River at San Pedro Macati.

Meanwhile, the Second Division was advancing north on the road to Caloocan. Colonel F. C. Little's Kansas regiment captured two strong earthworks and adjacent blockhouses. The Third Artillery, as infantry, battled another rebel position, finally capturing the breastworks with a bayonet charge.

The following day, Aguinaldo issued his most savage proclamation. All Americans—men, women, and children—were to be massacred. In addition, Chinese living in the islands were to be put to death and their property confiscated. Fortunately, the American advance was so swift that Aguinaldo was never able to put his order into effect.

On the morning of February 6, General Hale sent a request to General MacArthur for additional troops to hold his extended front while he advanced on the waterworks pumping station. It was imperative to capture the station before the Insurgents cut off the water supply to Manila.

That afternoon, Colonel Stotsenberg was placed in command of two battalions and moved out toward the waterworks—about four miles east of the reservoir. Two Colorado companies made up his advance guard, followed by four guns of the Utah Artillery. A Tennessee battalion was deployed on the extreme right, and a detachment of Twenty-third Infantry headed for Mariquina, about a mile north of the pumping station, to guard the left flank.

As the Americans advanced across a series of hills, the Utah Artillery shelled rebel positions ahead of the troops. At the foot of the second hill, the soldiers found the body of Surgeon Young. He had ridden through the Insurgent lines by mistake. Twelve empty revolver cartridges were found by his side—evidence of the fight he had put up against the Filipinos.

By five o'clock, the Insurgents had been routed from the waterworks, but enemy snipers on the American right flank were becoming a problem.

The next morning, the captured Spanish gunboat, *Laguna de Bay*, steamed up the Pasig River and shelled the sniper positions. Detachments of the Twentieth Infantry and Nebraska volunteers then swung south and drove the Insurgents toward the river. At the same time, a Wyoming battalion advanced on the enemy's front. Attacked on three sides, the rebels were driven inland, and the countryside was cleared of the enemy.

The Twenty-third Infantry surrounded Mariquina and white flags were observed flying from every house. The natives welcomed the troops with shouts of "Viva Americanos." However, like many of the villages, whoever was "pounding on the gates" at that particular time was in charge. The Filipinos were exceptionally well trained in the art of "riding the fence."

For the next couple of days, General Hale straightened his lines. He now occupied blockhouses 3 through 7, and had extended his front from the pumping station south to the Pasig River—a total of nine miles.

Meanwhile, train loads of Insurgents were noticed moving into Caloocan—twelve miles north of Manila. Among these troops was the infamous Seventy-third Filipino Regiment. During the battle for Manila, they deserted from the Spaniards, killed their Spanish officers, and joined Aguinaldo's army.

General Elwell Otis decided to attack the Insurgent stronghold as soon as possible. On February 10, he requested the assistance of Admiral Dewey's fleet and issued attack orders to General MacArthur.

At three o'clock that afternoon, the U.S.S. *Monadnock* and the U.S.S. *Charleston* began bombarding Caloocan from the sea, while the Sixth Artillery and Utah batteries opened fire on the rebel entrenchments.

The countryside between Manila and Caloocan was thick with banana groves, bamboo hedges, and rice fields—all of which afforded excellent cover for the Filipinos.

After the warships and land artillery had pounded the city for two hours, General Harrison Otis directed his brigade to advance. The Kansas, Montana, and Idaho volunteers moved forward on a wide front. They were supported by the Third Artillery and a detachment of Fourth Cavalry.

The Insurgents poured a blistering fire at the American line, but their aim was wild and misdirected. For many of the Filipino defenders, this was the first time that they had ever held a rifle in their hands.

Otis ordered his men not to answer the enemy Mausers until he gave the command. When the brigade neared the first line of rebel trenches, the signal was given to open fire.

The American volleys were accurate and deadly. The Filipinos deserted their breastworks and fled into the city. An officer of the Third Artillery stated: "We pushed forward in the face of enemy bullets as though they were snowballs."

The bewildered Insurgents attempted to regroup, but they suddenly discovered that they had been flanked by a Montana company. Major Bell's men had sneaked east without being detected and attacked the rebel's left flank. Bell then dashed north of the city to try to cut off any fleeing enemy troops.

The Kansas and Montana battalions jumped the abandoned trenches, raced forward, and drove into Caloocan. The city was ablaze as Aguinaldo's rear guard fought a desperate delaying action—giving their army a chance to escape into the surrounding hills.

By six o'clock, Caloocan and the Manila-Dagupan Railroad were in American hands. MacArthur was now able to move his division by rail to the Insurgent headquarters at Malabon. However, Aguinaldo abandoned the city on the following day and burned most of the town to the ground.

On February 11, an American naval force, commanded by Lieutenant Niblack of the U.S.S. *Boston*, established a beachhead on the island of Panay and fought its way to the town of Iloilo. An army battalion, under General M. P. Miller, was landed and forced its way through the city. The Insurgents set fire to Chinese homes and buildings. They also torched the American, British, and German consulates.

General Marcus Wright stated: "These victories were believed, for awhile, to have discouraged Aguinaldo, and overtures for a peaceful settlement were made to the American Eighth Corps commander. However, General Elwell Otis refused to consider any terms except unconditional surrender of all rebel forces, and their unqualified submission to the dictates of the United States Government.

"But Aguinaldo was a man of unbounded ambition. He was unwilling to relinquish his position as leader of the newly organized Philippine Republic, and elected to continue his war for independence.

"Aguinaldo reformed his shattered ranks and stirred up and encouraged other tribes of the archipelago to join the conflict against the American army of invasion. He succeeded so well, that natives in the islands of Mindanao, Cebu, and Luzon acknowledged allegiance to the rebel leader and flocked to his support."

Daily skirmishes occurred between American and Insurgent forces, but the Filipinos adopted hit-and-run guerrilla tactics—continually keeping the Eighth Army Corps off balance. The rebels would lure American detachments into the interior, beyond the range of Dewey's fleet—and to locations where it was difficult for troops to maneuver effectively.

On March 4, 1899, the Twenty-second Infantry Regiment reached the Philippines. Captain Jacob Kreps continued his diary: "The long tedious journey was at last drawing to an end. Corregidor Island was passed and our ship entered Manila Bay. Thoughts of a speedy release from this floating prison—and expectations of a pleasant tour of duty excited everyone. The transport's decks were crowded with happy, curious 'passengers.'

"The two hour ride from the mouth of the harbor to our anchorage seemed to take forever—but finally the masts of shipping appeared in the distance. We steamed past a German warship, which dipped her colors to the Stars and Stripes flying from our foremast. And we received the same courtesy from a natty Japanese cruiser and a formidable Englishman.

"A motor launch came alongside and an officer, standing in the boat, was immediately assailed by a volley of questions. We had received no news from the States for a month—but the ominous clouds of smoke on all sides of the bay aroused our curiosity. It certainly was not 'spring cleaning.'

"The officer's answers only confirmed my suspicions. Hostilities between our forces and the Filipinos had already commenced. A few days earlier, a strong Insurgent battalion from the north had entered Malabon, forded the swamps on General MacArthur's left flank, and attacked Manila. They set fire to the Santa Cruz and Tondo districts before being driven back to Malabon where they were firmly entrenched.

"Farewell to my hopes for a peaceful sojourn in our country's new possession."

The Twenty-second Infantry landed the next day and camped that night along the waterfront. In the morning, they moved to the barracks at Malate. The troops were given a week to rest and get their land-legs back before moving out to the south line of trenches.

General Hale's control of the waterworks was in jeopardy. His brigade was continually exposed to flank attacks from Pasig and vicinity. With the arrival of the Twenty-second Regiment, it was decided to put an end to the nuisance by driving the Insurgents from the north bank of the river. General Lloyd Wheaton was placed in charge of the operation as commander of a "Provisional Brigade" known as "Wheaton's Flying Column." The brigade was composed of the Twentieth and Twenty-second Infantries—two Washington battalions—seven Oregon companies—one platoon of the Sixth Artillery—and three troops of the Fourth Cavalry.

Wheaton's instructions were to drive the enemy beyond the town of Pasig, "striking him wherever found."

On the night of March 12, 1899, the brigade was formed and bivouacked to the rear of the American entrenchments extending from San Pedro Macati to the bay. Captain Kreps and Company M formed on the right flank of the Twenty-second Infantry line. To their extreme right was the Fourth Cavalry.

Jacob Kreps wrote in pencil and ink on water-stained pages: "On March 12, we marched to San Pedro Macati. Rain started to fall before we reached our destination. Company M passed a sister regiment—the men standing on one foot, then the other, attempting to keep dry—while, at the same time, trying to keep a fire going and fry bacon.

"After trudging across several muddy rice fields, we took our position a few hundred yards to the rear of the trenches. A short distance beyond, was a church occupied by an Oregon detachment. This veteran outfit consoled the rookies of the Twenty-second with such factious remarks as, 'You're up against the real thing now!'

"The rain kept up, more or less, all during the night. Everyone was miserable—especially the new recruits who were getting their first taste

Map 5.3
Insurgent-Controlled Towns South of the Pasig River

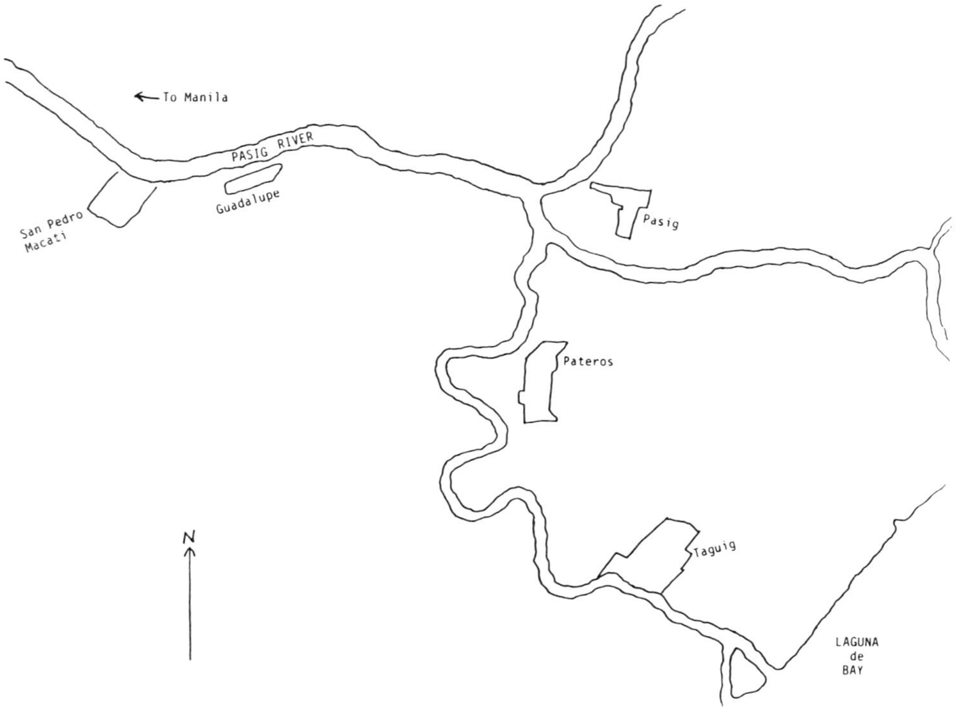

of field service. Many of the men were without cover. Very few took the trouble to put up their shelter tents—preferring to have the canvas between themselves and the ground—rather than between their bodies and the sky. However, I can't blame them. In a Philippine rainstorm, a shelter tent gives about as much protection as an equal size piece of wire netting."

Beyond the American positions, but within gunshot range, rose the Guadalupe ridge—a series of low bluffs that afforded the Insurgents excellent observation sites.

Captain Kreps continued his journal: "We were drenched to the skin, trying vainly to rest comfortably on the rough ground. The frowning cliff in front of us grimly promised death or frightful wounds—possibly during the night—surely in the morning. These depressing thoughts possessed the soldiers of Company M—the majority of whom were spending the first evening of their lives in discomfort and danger.

"And for the older soldiers too, this wet and soggy night had its effect. Memories of a mother or wife brought a strange choking sensation to the throat. But, when this was followed by thoughts of a little daughter—just old enough to remember 'Papa,' and a son still unable to toddle alone—the agony was almost too great to bear.

"The long dreary night finally drew to a close and the sun, shining in all its southern brilliance, chased away the gloomy shadows of darkness from the face of Mother Earth—and from the minds of the poor boys assembled here, in soldier uniforms, for the propagation of liberty."

At six o'clock on the morning of March 13, Wheaton's brigade moved forward by echelon from the right—the Twenty-second Infantry and Fourth Cavalry leading the way. The terrain in front of the Twenty-second's advance was rough and broken. Trees and bamboo thickets prevented a clear view of what lay ahead.

Suddenly, from their concealed positions on the cliffs, the Insurgents opened fire at long range. Captain Kreps recorded the incident in his diary: "The rookies of Company M heard a whistling noise and glanced curiously at each other—wondering if it was the sound of a lizard or some other animal. Then another whistle—and the men quickly realized that they were hearing their first hostile bullets. Heads dodged—soldiers darted for the nearest cover and hugged the ground.

"They later discovered, that if a bullet had time to sing a solo, it would be distant—too far away to do any harm. However, if it passed with a zip—a tree, mudbank, or stone wall were handy bulwarks to have around. The vicious pellets were never alone—they always had companions following them."

The Twenty-second Infantry continued to head the advance—enemy bullets constantly whizzing overhead, but by now, the youngsters of Company M had become accustomed to the sound—and the poor marksmanship of the Filipinos.

General Wheaton ordered the Fourth Cavalry detached from the line and directed them to make a wide detour toward the Pasig River in case the Insurgents retreated in that direction. Two companies of the Twenty-second were sent to assist the cavalry. The rest of the "Provisional Brigade" continued to apply pressure on the enemy and forced the rebels from their fortified positions on the Guadalupe ridge.

The Filipinos fell back—fighting stubbornly until they reached the river. Many of Aguinaldo's men surrendered—while others tried to swim the stream through a hail of bullets. Captain Kreps wrote: "We came upon seven Filipinos on the riverbank. They all surrendered except one plucky fellow. He threw his gun in the river and plunged in himself. Although the water around him was churned by bullets, I believe he succeeded in escaping.

"We rested an hour or so, filled our canteens, and had a light lunch—damn light in my case—two spoonfuls of uncooked canned tomatoes and a radish. However, the afternoon wasn't a total loss—I was treated to a drink of whiskey.

"After lunch, Company D was also placed under my command, and I was given orders to clear the way forward. My assignment was to occupy a series of bluffs along the river—opposite the town of Pasig. The exact distance to these cliffs was not known—nor whether they were defended by the rebels.

"We moved out cautiously, but evidently not fast enough for Colonel Egbert and General Wheaton. They urged the rookies on with such fervor that the head of my column crowded on the heels of the advance guard.

"We soon approached a stretch of road that was dangerously visible from across the river and the city of Pasig. At this spot, the river formed a T with the town on the left. The cliffs we were to seize were located in the angle formed by the stem of the T and the right arm of the river.

"Company M had no sooner reached the road, when we were scattered by a rapid fire volley from the opposite bank. There never was a pathway paved with human bodies as quickly as this one—but miraculously nobody was hit.

"About thirty yards ahead, I noticed a steep embankment perpendicular to the river. I immediately occupied the position with ten volunteers. After summoning the rest of the company, we opened fire on the Insurgents. Under cover of our barrage, I directed Lieutenant Isaac Newell and Company D to move forward and take shelter beneath the projecting lip of a cliff across the road from us.

"However, we still had not accomplished our mission. I knew that the Filipinos were within gunshot range—and possibly on the path ahead. Therefore, I sent Company D to skirt the high ground and come in on the flank of any enemy troops that might be dug in on the bluffs. Company M would continue to advance along the road.

"We crept forward, slowly and carefully—rifles at the ready. A grove of trees and banana plants soon obstructed our view—but also hid us from the rebels. The trail suddenly curved sharply, and for about a hundred yards the roadway was cut through a hill of solid rock. The stone walls rose thirty feet on both sides of the path. At the far end of the gorge, the curve straightened out and came into full view of the opposite bank.

"I decided to take a few men and investigate. We sneaked through the cut until I noticed the enemy positions across the river. The Insurgent trenches controlled this part of the road—and we soon discovered that they were manned by sharpshooters.

"My troops were spotted, and several straw hats popped into view above the enemy earthworks. Each hat represented a puff of smoke—a bang—then the splatter of a bullet on the rock wall.

"We quickly ran for cover—out of sight from the enemy riflemen. That is, all except Private William Reinhardt. Several times the youngster stepped out into the middle of the road—deliberately knelt, aimed, and fired—then dashed back to the tunnel to reload. He tried this once too often and was shot in the foot."

General Wheaton and the rest of the brigade hurried east to support Captain Kreps.

Companies M and D both reached the bluffs at about the same time. Jacob Kreps described the action: "The firing was brisk and accurate on the part of the rebels across the river. Two men from Company D were shot through the head, and a tree, directly behind Lieutenant Newell, was struck by five bullets.

"The *Laguna de Bay* was called in to bolster our attack. The gunboat was commanded by Captain Grant. He managed to maneuver the vessel past the wreck of the scuttled *Cebu*, and succeeded in driving the Insurgents from their trenches.

Company M had been under heavy fire for the first time during this engagement. The men were exhausted. They slept undisturbed that night and had a good rest—surprisingly it didn't rain."

Wheaton's brigade occupied the high ground across from Pasig. Two guns of the Sixth Artillery, under Lieutenant Scott, pounded the enemy defenses. One battalion of the Twenty-second, including Company M, were sent ahead toward Pateros. They attacked a detachment of fleeing Insurgents and drove them beyond Taguig. The Twenty-second Infantry then reformed and bivouacked on the cliffs across from Pateros.

The following day, a battalion of Twentieth Infantry, under Major Rogers, crossed the river and stormed Pasig. An Oregon company crossed below the city and attacked the Filipinos as they attempted to escape east of the town.

Captain Kreps recorded one disturbing incident: "At this time, previously and subsequently, there was a great deal of looting and plundering—to the lasting disgrace of our uniform. It was rumored that companies of the Washington volunteers had fifty thousand dollars on deposit in Hong Kong banks."

The Insurgents were firmly entrenched in bamboo thickets across the river from Pateros. A Washington battalion, commanded by Major John Weisenburger, traversed the water in canoes and assaulted the enemy breastworks. The rebels were routed and burned the town as they retreated.

The Twenty-second Regiment remained in bivouac until March 18. Jacob Kreps narrated: "This day [March 18] was the hottest day of my life. The heat was unbearable. Squads from every company were sent out to locate water and provisions—leaving our battalion with less than two hundred men in camp.

"During this period, the men grudgingly accepted the hardship of life in the Philippines. Every night, heavy typhoon rains poured down on the regimental encampment—shelter tents were useless. Toward morning, officers and men—drenched and shivering—rose from their muddy beds and sat around campfires until the sun finally appeared and dried the clothes on their backs."

That afternoon, a large Insurgent force appeared in the vicinity of Taguig. They established their position on the high cliffs west of the city and attacked a nearby Washington company. Captain Kreps described the events that quickly followed: "About three o'clock, our depleted battalion was placed under the command of Captain Frank Jones. We were ordered to move out and attempt to rescue the besieged company. However, our directive stated for us to proceed down to the river and move forward along the bank. I protested and asked permission to advance across the high ground. General Wheaton denied my request. I considered his order irresponsible. It would have been much safer advancing along the ridge. As it was, we could—and did—head into a trap.

"Companies D, E, and G formed the front line of the battalion with Company M in reserve. After marching two miles, firing was heard. We could make out the Washington outfit delivering volleys—but there was no sign of the enemy.

"Scouts suddenly brought word that there were about eight hundred Insurgents to our front. I hoped that the size of the rebel force was exaggerated—if correct, we were outnumbered four to one.

"As we pushed on ahead, the terrain became rough and rockstrewn—then cliffs emerged on our right and left flanks. Within a few minutes we found ourselves cornered in a horseshoe shaped depression. High ground surrounded us on all sides—except at the narrow entrance to the shoe.

"The lead companies had proceeded about five hundred yards when the 'music' began. A hailstorm of Mauser bullets rained down on the troops. Further progress was impossible. The men dashed for cover and commenced firing back at the enemy. But our front line was suffering heavy casualties and ammunition was beginning to run short.

"Captain Jones shouted orders for the battalion to retreat from the trap, and directed Company M to protect the withdrawal. However, the sudden wild, disorganized rush of men descended upon my troops so rapidly that our company became intermingled with the returning firing line. There was a great deal of confusion as the retiring soldiers crowded through the narrow opening of the horseshoe—while, at the same time, we were trying to move past them to the front. During the melee, Jones was shot and I assumed command of the battalion.

"It was a madhouse of frustration. We were afraid to fire at the

Filipinos for fear of hitting our own troops as they attempted to flee the trap. Meanwhile, Insurgent bullets pelted down on us in a pitiless shower. Three of my men were shot, including Henry Johnson.

"I was finally able to reform Company M as a line of skirmishers, and began a rapid fire assault on the enemy positions. By the time that the rest of the battalion was clear of the horseshoe, the Filipinos began to retreat. In a little over an hour, our battalion had lost twenty men—killed or wounded."

It was nearly dark when the soldiers of Company M returned to their tents. The sun had set, and a full moon looked down upon the litter bearers hauling the dead and wounded from the battlefield. The long line of stretchers—stopping every few minutes to change carriers—dragged its slow course back to camp.

Jacob Kreps was tired, bitter, and depressed after the furious battle, and he eloquently expressed his feelings in the pages of his notebook: "I searched the hospital tents until I located Johnson. An enemy bullet had entered just over the left eye and passed completely through his head. The youngster never regained consciousness. Johnson's brief service in the Army of the United States was over—but his dedication will not be soon forgotten.

"The history of a soldier in the regular army, or any soldier for that matter, is the story of his organization while he is affiliated with it.

"The hero is usually of newspaper manufacture—and remains a hero for possibly three editions. The soldier who falls in combat needs no such notoriety. If his company or regiment never disgraces its flag—but only adds to the brightness of its colors—this honor is shared with his comrades.

"However, what good is honor to Johnson now? His body lies on the island of Luzon—sacrificed to a policy not to be criticized by the soldier, but which has as its objective the subjugation of a people fighting for their liberty.

"Henry Johnson died—not in defense of his country—but rather because duty summoned him to that rugged, rocky spot near Laguna de Bay where the messenger of death was waiting. No sentiment nor feelings motivated his actions—only the stern obligation to flag and country, ready to meet any foe, domestic or foreign. Ready to obey the legal orders of his superiors. This is, and always will be, the function of the 'regular soldier.'"

Jacob F. Kreps as a cadet at the U.S. Military Academy, West Point.
Courtesy of the U.S. Army Military History Institute.

Sioux Indian dance at the Rosebud Agency, Dakota Territory. *Courtesy of the U.S. Army Military History Institute.*

Officers of the Twenty-second Infantry Regiment, August 1892. Front row, left to right: Lockwood, Murphy, Hutton, McCammon, Page, Theaker, and Patterson. Back row, left to right: Phillips, Lindsey (unidentified), Jones, Kreps, Hamilton, and Ballance.

Courtesy of National Archives: 111-SC-98064.

Colonel Jacob F. Kreps, circa 1915.
Courtesy of the Arizona Historical Society, #77350, and the U.S. Army Military History Institute.

Generals Garcia, Lawton, Ludlow, and Chaffee inspecting the American lines at El Caney.
Courtesy of the U.S. Army Military History Institute.

Wounded arriving at the First Division Field Hospital at El Caney.
Courtesy of the U.S. Army Military History Institute.

General Joseph Wheeler leads his troops inland after landing at Daiquiri, Cuba. *Courtesy of the U.S. Army Military History Institute.*

Emilio Aguinaldo.
Courtesy of the National Archives: 111-SC-93268.

Seventh Infantry firing line at San Juan Hill, July 9, 1898.
Courtesy of the National Archives: 111-84847.

Twenty-second Infantry private of Company E, Philippine Islands.
Courtesy of the U.S. Army Military History Institute.

Noncommissioned officers of the Twenty-second Infantry Regiment in the Philippines. *Courtesy of the U.S. Army Military History Institute.*

Twenty-second Infantry Regiment quarters in a thatched hut behind a church at Balanga, Philippine Islands.
Courtesy of the U.S. Army Military History Institute.

Twenty-second Infantry bivouac at Camp Marahui, Mindanao.
Courtesy of the U.S. Army Military History Institute.

Twenty-second Infantry and Fourteenth Cavalry crossing the Taraca River in Mindanao. *Courtesy of the U.S. Army Military History Institute.*

Twenty-second Infantry firing line near the Pasig River.
Courtesy of the National Archives: 111-SS-81100.

Twenty-second Infantry entering Malolos, March 31, 1899.
Courtesy of the U.S. Army Military History Institute.

Chapter Six

THE MALOLOS CAMPAIGN

On March 18, 1899, General Henry Lawton replaced General Anderson as commander of the First Division.

The following day, Wheaton's "Provisional Brigade" deployed south, with the Twenty-second Infantry formed on the right of the line. Using the left as a pivot, the brigade attacked the Insurgents south of Taguig and drove them down the shore of Laguna de Bay.

Captain Kreps recalled: "We marched twelve miles in extended order during the swinging movement. The heat was suffocating. On the return march, our already battered battalion valiantly endured the unrelenting sun. Men collapsed from exhaustion and were carried into camp by their comrades—whose condition was not much better.

"Near Taguig we could see the ghastly evidence of the previous day's engagement—many bloated, foul-smelling corpses wearing Insurgent uniforms. Considering the extreme care exercised by the Filipinos in removing their dead, the number left on the battlefield showed the heavy losses we inflicted upon them."

On March 20, General Wheaton's troops were ordered to return to Manila. The mission of the expedition had been thoroughly accomplished. During the week's campaign, every enemy position attacked by the brigade had been captured—and the rebel forces had been dispersed and demoralized.

In the meantime, Aguinaldo had firmly established his headquarters at Malolos—about twenty-five miles northwest of Manila. He contin-

Map 6.1
Towns and Rivers on the Route to Malolos

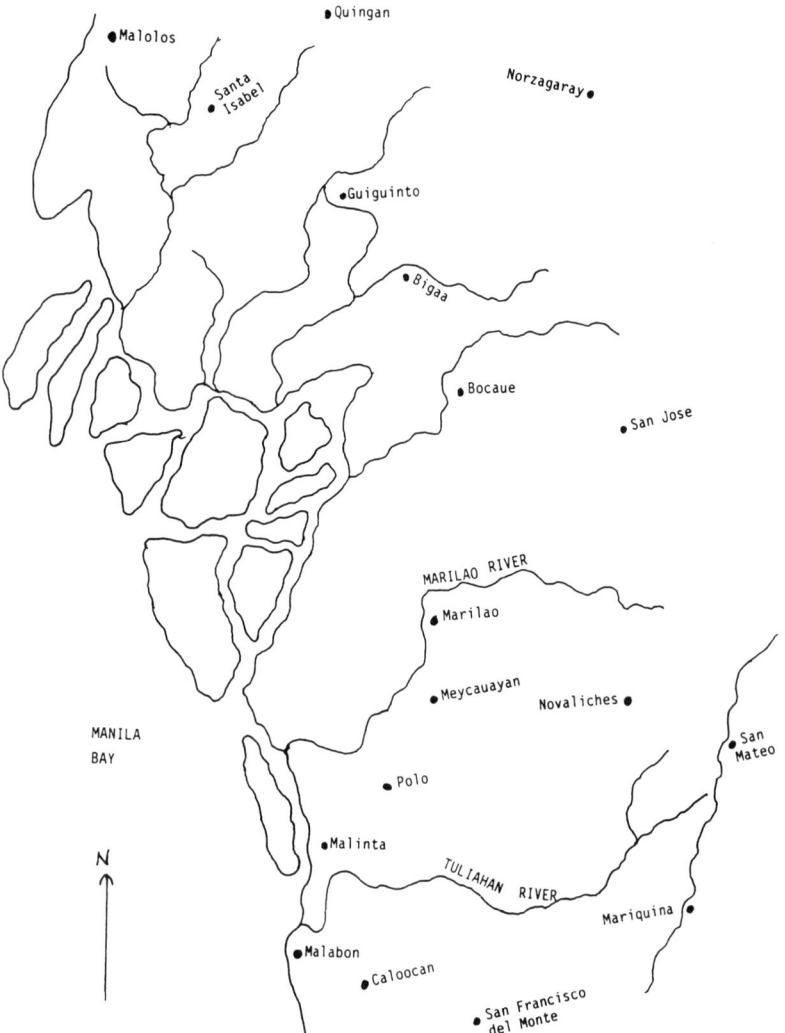

ued to receive funds by collecting taxes and from donations of wealthy Filipinos. This money was used to purchase weapons and ammunition from countries "friendly" to the United States. The strength of the Insurgent army was estimated at thirty thousand men—many of whom were natives from the hill country. They received no military training and were ignorant of modern warfare. The Filipinos were marched into a trench, handed a gun, and told in which direction to shoot.

General Elwell Otis conferred with MacArthur and Dewey. They decided that, if the rebel army could be surrounded and captured—along with Aguinaldo—then the rebellion would come to a satisfactory conclusion.

Near the end of March, General MacArthur's Second Division faced north. Its lines extended from a point on Manila Bay near Caloocan, east to the La Loma Church, and then south to the Pasig River opposite San Pedro Macati.

The Insurgent entrenchments stretched along the front of MacArthur's division—from Polo, through Novaliches, to the Nanca River.

In preparation for an attack on Malolos, the Second Division was reorganized. A Third Brigade was created from General Hale's command and newly arrived reinforcements. This unit included the Wyoming and Minnesota volunteers and the Seventeenth Infantry Regiment. The brigade was placed under the command of General R. H. Hall, and assigned to guard the reservoir and waterworks.

General Wheaton's brigade—comprising the Twenty-second Infantry, the Third Infantry, and an Oregon battalion—was transferred to MacArthur's division and stationed to the left of the American line at Manila Bay. To Wheaton's right was General Harrison Otis with the Montana and Kansas regiments, and two battalions of the Third Artillery as infantry. General Hale's brigade formed the right of the line, and consisted of the Pennsylvania, South Dakota, Colorado, and Nebraska volunteers.

MacArthur now had approximately twelve thousand men under his command for the operation against Malolos. Lawton's First Division was directed to hold the rebels in check south of the Pasig River.

The American plan of attack was to advance north, parallel to the shore of the bay. The terrain was swampy and cut up by numerous interconnecting tidal estuaries called "esteros." From the marshlands the ground rose to a line of foothills and then flattened out to a broad plain, intersected by many rivers.

The Insurgent defenses were along the banks of the rivers that flowed into the bay. The countryside was densely populated and cultivated with rice fields. There were several roads traversing the open country, but most of them were impassable for field artillery.

MacArthur planned to advance along an eight-mile front and on both sides of the Manila-Dagupan Railroad tracks. Admiral Dewey was directed to dispose his fleet to cover the bay flank of the division and have his ships available to transport soldiers to a point north of Malolos for an attack on the enemy rear.

On March 24, General Wheaton's brigade moved to its assigned position. The enemy lines were about a thousand yards to the front, and the rebels were in high spirits. Captain Kreps related: "All during the night, the Filipinos sang and celebrated. They fired volleys in our direction, but we were under strict orders not to return the salvos. Bonfires blazed along their lines. The Insurgents danced around the flames and mockingly exposed themselves to our riflemen. They shouted taunts and insults, played our calls on their bugles, and their voices imitated our commands."

At daylight, the Utah Artillery opened fire on the enemy entrenchments, and General MacArthur gave the order for his troops to advance.

Wheaton's brigade moved out first. The Twenty-second Infantry, commanded by Colonel Harry C. Egbert, was on the right flank of the brigade. A battalion of Third Infantry, under Captain Cooke, covered the center, with two companies on either side of the railroad embankment. Colonel Summers and his Oregon detachment moved forward on the left—along the shoreline separating Malabon from the mainland.

The Third Battalion of the Twenty-second was ordered forward, in echelon, to protect the left flank of Harrison Otis' brigade. General Hale was directed to swing his regiments left and force the enemy toward the sea.

Jacob Kreps narrated: "The Insurgents were in force along their entrenchments, and opened up with a heavy Mauser barrage. At first their firing was accurate and incessant. However, as we continued to advance, it soon decreased in volume and accuracy. The rebels either dropped their weapons and fled, or else shot unaimed volleys over our heads.

"In marked contrast, the fire of our men remained strong despite casualties—and even more accurate as the enemy offered better targets.

Before we had covered half the distance between the opposing line of trenches, the Filipinos abandoned their rifle pits and fled.

"However, the terrain was such that they were able to make numerous stands. And under the natural protection of these positions, they fired rapidly with telling effect. But they could not withstand the uninterrupted forward progress of our columns. American methods of warfare do not permit hours of fighting from entrenched positions—and without losses to either combatant."

The Twenty-second Infantry drove the Insurgents back from row after row of defenses. The rebels retreated stubbornly, abandoning their territory only after suffering heavy casualties.

By noon, Wheaton's brigade had pushed the Filipinos across the Tuliahan River. Two guns of the Utah Artillery were brought up to within nine hundred yards of the railroad trestle that bridged the wide stream. For more than an hour they shelled enemy blockhouses and rifle pits on the river's north bank, but the rebel defenses were formidable, and the American troops bivouacked along the south shore of the Tuliahan for the remainder of the day.

General Hale's brigade also ran into stubborn resistance. The South Dakota and Pennsylvania regiments were pinned down by enemy Mauser fire from strong Insurgent barricades on the Masambong road. Lieutenant Naylor's Utah Artillery battery was finally called in and vigorously bombarded the rebel breastworks. A bayonet charge was called, and the soldiers, hollering like a thousand banshees, dashed across the rice fields and swarmed over the enemy entrenchments.

A news correspondent wrote in his account of the assault: "The sight behind the breastworks was appalling. Filipinos were in all attitudes of pain—their life blood seeping into the land they sought to free. Some called for water—some for cigarettes—and some for death. The rice fields are brown and unsown—but next year, how this red rain will nourish a harvest!"

The Nebraska troops advanced along the banks of the San Juan River and, in hand-to-hand combat, battled their way into San Francisco del Monte. The town was burned to the ground during the vicious engagement.

General Hale's dog-tired soldiers continued their hurry-up march toward Novaliches. Smoke from the flaming huts of Cabataon and Talinapa marked the route of their relentless advance.

However, the rapid pace and scorching heat soon began to take their toll on the volunteers. Stretcher bearers were kept on the run, picking up the limp bodies of men who had collapsed from heat exhaustion.

Hale was forced to abandon his attack on Novaliches. He swung his brigade toward the Tuliahan River and moved northwest along the south bank. He intended to cross the river at the site of an uncompleted bridge, but ran into heavy enemy fire from the north shore. Naylor's Utah battery was again brought up and pounded the rebels back from their defensive positions. General Hale bivouacked his troops along the riverbank for the night.

Because of the Second Division's difficulty in maneuvering across the rice fields and through thick jungles of bamboo, it became apparent to MacArthur that his original plans could not be carried out. Although the enemy's center had been broken, it was impossible for his army to advance rapidly enough to envelop Aguinaldo's troops.

On the morning of March 26, reconnaissance revealed that the only path suitable for artillery and supply trains was a hard-packed dirt road that passed through the city of Malinta. The town was to the immediate front of the Twenty-second Infantry.

Meanwhile, the Oregon battalion, which had been heading north along the bayshore, ran into fierce opposition between Malabon and the Tuliahan River. General Marcus Wright stated: "The Insurgents were well concealed in the woods to our front. They held their fire until the Oregon soldiers had approached to within two hundred yards, and then unleashed a murderous volley. The American line never wavered. Shouting a war cry, our troops charged the thicket—their slashing bayonets ripping through the enemy entrenchments. The Filipinos panicked and ran off in all directions—like the Indians did on the western frontier.

"The Oregon volunteers advanced to the outskirts of Malabon before rebel resistance stiffened. The natives fought like demons—at times leaping from their trenches and rushing the Americans.

"Despite increasing Mauser fire, and suicidal charges, the Oregon battalion held its ground. A call for reinforcements brought Captain Cooke with a detachment of Third Infantry. After the arrival of fresh troops, the assault on Malabon was renewed. The enemy defense broke, and the Filipinos fled into the city—torching the town as we pursued them through the streets."

The Twenty-second Infantry marched a short distance to the right and forded the Tuliahan. Once across the river, the regiment came under heavy attack from Aguinaldo's rear guard. Colonel Egbert formed his line perpendicular to the river in order to flank the Insurgent earthworks along the railroad tracks.

The Twenty-second headed north—the First Battalion moving forward to scout the terrain ahead. Captain Kreps described the action: "The rebels were strongly entrenched on commanding ground eight hundred yards south of Malinta. These rifle pits were attacked and quickly captured. But a short distance beyond stood a stone church which was protected by a breast high masonry wall—bristling with Mausers. It was here that the Insurgents hoped to check our advance. The ground in front of the church had a natural slope—broken only by a few rice paddies. About every hundred yards of the approach was marked by palm streamers flying from tall bamboos.

"The enemy poured a galling fire upon the scouting battalion and forced the soldiers to seek shelter in the empty trenches and rice fields. Our return volleys, directed at the crest of the wall, only seemed to increase the intensity of the rebel barrage.

"Colonel Egbert ordered the rest of the regiment forward. When they reached the front, the men hit the dirt and began pouring a well directed fire on the Filipino defenders. The battle raged for twenty minutes, then Egbert led a bayonet charge—routing the enemy. The colonel was killed in the victorious assault."

When the Twenty-second Infantry entered the churchyard, they found large quantities of ammunition behind the wall. The regiment bivouacked at Malinta and waited for the Oregon battalion to arrive.

In the meantime, General Hale's brigade had also crossed the Tuliahan and deployed north. About three o'clock, they came up against a strong enemy force south of Meycauayan. A South Dakota battalion, commanded by Major Howard, sneaked into the woods on the right and flanked the Insurgents—driving them back all along the front.

However, the rest of the brigade came under hot fire from rebels entrenched in bamboo thickets near the railroad bridge. General Hale rode across his front line to ascertain the enemy positions and was shot in the knee. He bandaged his own wound, and directed Captain Krayenbuhl to bring up a battalion and flank the enemy trenches. Krayenbuhl was killed while carrying out the order.

Colonel Stotsenberg took command and, with his Nebraska troops, succeeding in flanking the rebels. He then joined up with the South Dakota battalion and drove the Insurgents into the jungle.

The following morning, the brigades of Generals Hale and Harrison Otis advanced toward the Marilao River. Wheaton's regiments were ordered to cover the railroad and keep the tracks open for the movement of troops and supplies.

About noon, the brigades of Hale and Otis bumped into a large Insurgent force that was entrenched south of Marilao. The rebel army was commanded by Aguinaldo and three of his generals—Garcia, Torres, and Pacheco.

The Filipinos boldly advanced to meet MacArthur's division. The Nebraska, South Dakota, and Pennsylvania volunteers were to the right of the American line—while the Kansas, Montana, and Third Artillery detachments were on the left.

General Wright stated: "This was the first time that the Filipinos attacked in battle formation. Our men held their fire until the enemy was within four hundred yards—then the command to commence firing was signaled all along the front. There was a deafening roar of field artillery and the explosions from a thousand rifles. The rebel line broke, and Aguinaldo's troops deserted in mass confusion.

"We could see the Insurgent officers trying to halt the flight of their men—but without success. No control could be established against the steady advance of our troops. Filipino prisoners, who were captured during the engagement, declared that their superiors stood behind them with whips and lashed the unwilling men—forcing them to hold their positions. This fact was supported by evidence of marks upon the bodies of the rebels who were killed where they stood. Aguinaldo was also accused of sentencing men to death who refused to fight, or were caught after fleeing from a battle."

The Insurgents escaped across the Marilao River. Cheering wildly, the South Dakota troops waded waist-deep through the stream and charged up the opposite bank—driving the enemy into the wooded hills beyond.

When the Second Division entered the town of Marilao, they found the city deserted. A supply train from Manila soon arrived with rations and ammunition to continue the offensive.

On the morning of March 29, General MacArthur brought the Twenty-second Regiment up to the front to lead the advance. The Filipinos had retreated in the direction of Malolos—tearing up sections of railroad track and burning several small villages. All along their line of march, the soldiers of the Second Division noticed unfinished enemy trenches. It was evident that the rebels were not prepared for the rapid American drive.

General Wright remarked: "It would be ludicrous to deny that our army commanders had many anxious moments. The resistance of the Filipinos was stubborn—and their fighting quality has proven to be clever, courageous, and unremitting. Our advantages have been due to discipline, determination, and control exerted against a cunning foe.

"The conflicts were always in favor of the Americans—but without decisive results. Aguinaldo personally commanded his army with great skill. For, although defeated at every point where a stand was made, he prevented a disastrous route—and succeeded in drawing off the majority of his forces toward Malolos."

The Insurgents had relied upon stopping MacArthur at the Marilao River—failing there, they withdrew beyond Bocaue and established their defenses east of Bulacan.

Jacob Kreps wrote in his diary: "We had expected strong resistance when we reached Bocaue. But evidently Aguinaldo was unwilling to risk another confrontation with our army. The city was a wasteland—not a single rebel was to be seen.

"Friendly natives informed us that the Insurgents had murdered twenty Chinese who protested the destruction of their property. The retreating Filipinos were accompanied by a large number of women and children. A group of Spanish prisoners was driven along in front of the fleeing columns. The Insurgents were very careful to prevent their escape—hoping that a hefty ransom would be paid for their release—or that better peace terms might be offered upon the condition of setting the Spaniards free."

General MacArthur's troops advanced steadily toward Malolos—using pontoon bridges to cross the many streams. All along the line of march, however, the rebels constantly harassed the flanks of the American brigades.

When the Second Division arrived at Bigaa, the enemy rear guard set fire to the bridge leading into town and ripped up a hundred feet of railroad track, but the fire was quickly extinguished and the track easily repaired.

Captain Kreps commented: "Our forced marches usually commenced after daylight—since the morning hours in the tropics are the coolest.

The afternoon hours from four to six are also favorable. Accordingly, we rested until half-past three, then headed north from Bigaa. We reached the Guiguinto River about five o'clock."

The following morning, March 30, MacArthur's division crossed the Guiguinto. The army rested a few hours in the jungle before resuming its march to Malolos.

General Hale's brigade suddenly encountered a strong rebel force entrenched along a wooded area to the right of the railroad. His troops were caught in the open, and the hidden enemy unleashed a withering fire into the advancing columns. The Nebraskans were hit hard, and losses were also sustained by the Pennsylvania and Dakota detachments.

Hale rapidly deployed his brigade and charged the Insurgent positions. However, Aguinaldo's soldiers made a planned withdrawal, from one line of trenches to another, before scattering into the hills.

General MacArthur and his staff walked abreast of the Filipino assault, and were fired upon by sharpshooters hidden in the trees. Although bullets kicked up dirt on all sides of the officers, MacArthur did not blink an eye.

The Second Division bivouacked about two miles from Malolos, but throughout the night, the Americans were subjected to infiltrating attacks and sniper fire.

Jacob Kreps continued his journal: "When morning arrived, the weather was clear. The bright sunlight made the rich vegetation appear in glorious colors. While across the intervening lowlands toward the sea, there was an ineffable calm and shimmering haze of indescribable grandeur.

"Friendly natives reported that the Insurgents were prepared to defend their capital at Malolos as a political necessity. Our reconnaissance disclosed formidable earthworks and a large number of rebel soldiers. We made preparations for a battle of considerable proportions.

"Five battalions of regulars, including two battalions of the Twenty-second were brought forward to the front to support General [Harrison] Otis and his advance brigade.

"At seven o'clock, the peaceful scene was interrupted by cannon booms on the right. The Third Artillery opened the engagement, and began throwing a heavy stream of shells into the enemy entrenchments. The Utah battery quickly joined the action—followed in a half-hour with a charge by the South Dakota, Nebraska, and Kansas volunteers. They swept along both sides of the railroad tracks—over open fields, through thickets, and across streams until they reached the main line of rebel trenches south of the city.

"Our regiment followed, moving out in successive rows of skirmishers. From their superior positions, the Insurgents opened a spirited fire. But, our approach was marked by a series of natural obstacles—swamps, lagoons, marshes, bamboo thickets, and dense banana groves.

"Despite the impediments, we forged ahead in perfect order. The general plan of the battle, and its execution, were typical examples of strategy and military skill."

For nearly two hours, the Filipinos offered tenacious resistance, but failed to stop the American assault. The fighting raged hand-to-hand through the city streets. The town erupted in flames as the rebels set fires to block the advance of MacArthur's forces.

General Wright reported: "The Insurgent breastworks were well constructed—and had they been defended by a thousand such fighting soldiers as our own, might have repulsed a force ten times as great.

"But, the Filipinos, while brave, lacked the genius and indomitable dash of trained veterans. And also, without modern artillery, they could not withstand the assault charges of our troops—or the hail of bursting shells that broke devastatingly over their heads."

The fiery scene within the city was appalling. Hundreds of terrified, panic-stricken Chinese were screaming for mercy and striving to save their possessions. The pleading cries of women and children pierced the air with appeals for help. Chaos was everywhere as the suffocating heat from flames and smoke continued to engulf the dying town.

A Kansas officer recalled: "We charged down the main street of Malolos until we encountered a barricade defended by a small squad of Filipinos—intent on sacrificing themselves to cover the escape of their comrades.

"The rebels fired three volleys into our ranks, then fled. Colonel Funston rushed the barrier. Swinging his hat, he scrambled to the top of the rampart and shouted for his men to follow him in pursuit of the enemy."

By nine o'clock, all Insurgent opposition had ceased, and the entire Second Division marched into the city. Marcus Wright described the shocking scene of destruction that greeted General MacArthur: "When the rebels abandoned their capital, desolation was everywhere. Only two hours before, the town had some pretension of elegance. The Governor's Palace was a building of architectural beauty, and the home of the governing congress of the new republic. I had been informed that its decorations and furnishings were more luxurious than one might expect. The Filipinos admired this stately edifice. To them, it was the very enshrinement of their hopes for independence.

"It must have been, therefore, with deepest sorrow that they applied the torch to preserve it from profanation by their enemies. And, we might well imagine their grief, when fleeing for their lives, they looked back to see boiling clouds of smoke—rising with flashes of flame—that marked the now gutted hole where their proud capitol building had once stood."

American losses during the attack on Malolos were light. This was mainly due to poor marksmanship on the part of the Insurgents, and the fact that many of the Filipinos were unfamiliar with their weapons—firing at random and without discipline.

As the rebels retreated from the city, they destroyed several miles of railroad track to hinder MacArthur's pursuit. The Insurgents not only removed rails from the roadbed, but carried them into the woods, or threw them into streams, where they could not be easily recovered.

The entire route of the enemy withdrawal was a scene of devastation. Burned villages and rotting corpses marked the trail. General Wright continued: "Although defeated at every point, the Filipinos never lost their determination to resist. When it became evident that it was impossible to hold Malolos against the Americans, several prominent citizens pleaded with the rebels to surrender the city and thus save many lives and avoid the destruction of property. But, instead of granting their wishes, Aguinaldo's lieutenants executed the petitioners, demonstrating to the populace that the Insurgents intended to contest every foot of Philippine soil."

Emilio Aguinaldo was proving to be even more clever than General Elwell Otis had supposed. The rebel leader had foreseen the result of MacArthur's attack on Malolos, and on March 29, the self-proclaimed president of the Philippines fled with the main body of his troops into the mountainous jungle. He stationed a token defensive force of a few thousand men in the capital to cover his retreat.

Aguinaldo had not only managed to escape, but his army was still virtually intact. A sizable portion of the Insurgent forces retained their conventional organization and attempted to stem the American advance—while others were scattered in small bands throughout northern Luzon and adopted guerrilla tactics.

Captain Kreps narrated: "By his own acts, Aguinaldo's retreat from Caloocan to Malolos had been a path of fire and destruction. Noncombatants were driven from their homes, and their property destroyed by an army whose leaders expounded liberty and the fatherland. At Malolos, the rebels were forced to flee before they could accomplish the customary vandalism and looting of their own people.

"The Philippine countryside is nature's perfect paradise. North from Malolos, the land rises in gently undulating ridges. Fertile plains are broken by hedgerows of bamboos, banana, and acacia trees. The eye rests with grateful repose on the soft yellow flower of the amargosa—or welcomes the effective red blaze of the bougainvilla.

"But now, the waving grass, ripe for the sickle, will never be garnered. And fruit, that was ready to be plucked, has already been trampled under foot. Farmers, who should have been reaping the results of their labor, or preparing the soil, were summoned by the fiery cross of Aguinaldo. And soon thereafter they watched the smoking ruins of their homes from adjacent hillsides—unable to understand why this evil curse had been visited upon them.

"But this was war—grim, gaunt, inexorable—that spares nothing, and destroys without limit with blood-craving instruments of hate. The Filipinos had been driven from their capital—whose resistance, inspired by Aguinaldo's bootless ambition, had brought this grief upon their land."

Chapter Seven

THE LAGUNA DE BAY AND SAN MIGUEL CAMPAIGNS

The successful conclusion of the Malolos campaign found the Eighth Army Corps flushed with victory. Hardships of the expedition were forgotten amid the rejoicing and mistaken belief that the capture of Aguinaldo's capital meant the end of the insurrection.

On April 6, 1899, the Twenty-second Infantry was assigned to General Lawton's command. The regiment occupied a line of trenches extending from Pasay to San Pedro Macati—the southernmost line held by the First Division.

Jacob Kreps wrote: "The enemy forces were mainly made up of rookies who had never been under fire before. And, since we were under strict orders not to return the rebel Mauser fire, their bravery knew no bounds. The Insurgents continually made hourly attacks upon some part of the regiment's line—and at night their trenches sounded like a full-scale war was taking place.

"It was the sort of warfare that robs men of sleep, strains their nerves, and makes them fret because of forced inactivity. It was a warfare that demanded intense watchfulness and vigilance—but promised no rewards of victory."

While the Twenty-second Infantry stewed and complained, Lawton was busy putting together an expedition to clear the enemy from the shores of Laguna de Bay.

The terrain was beautiful rolling country and was densely populated. The district was important to Aguinaldo as a source of supplies and

Map 7.1
The Laguna de Bay Area

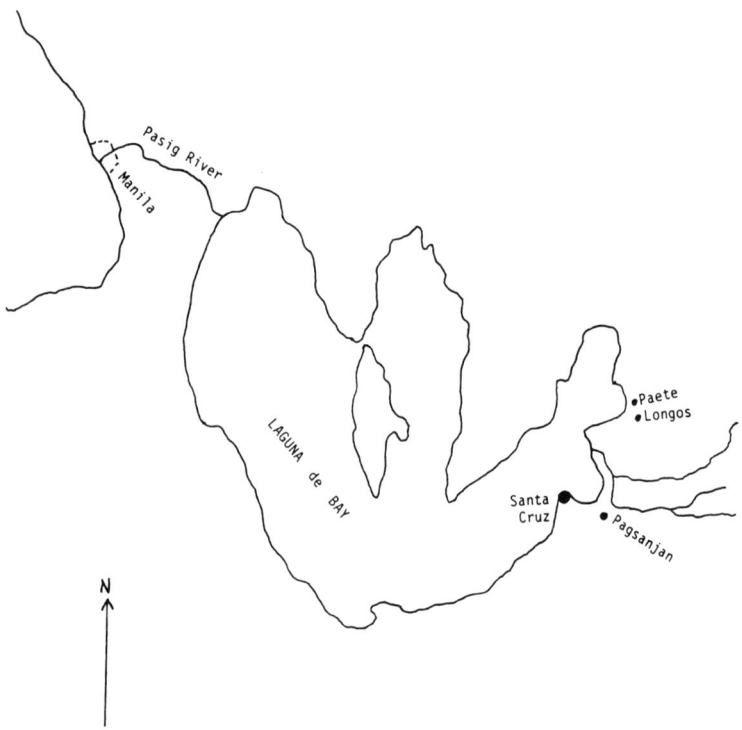

also afforded the rebels a point from which to make flank attacks against American outposts guarding the waterworks.

General Lawton's orders were to seize several enemy motor launches and barges, and to capture the city of Santa Cruz—the Insurgent's fortified bastion on the lake. The First Division would then swing back overland toward Manila Bay and crush the rebel forces at Paranaque.

Major Weisenburger, of the Washington volunteers, was placed in command of the expeditionary brigade. His troops were equipped in light marching order. Each man carried 200 rounds of ammunition and rations for ten days.

The terrain on either side of the Pasig River from Manila to Laguna de Bay—a distance of ten miles—consisted of rich rice fields that bordered the river as far east as San Pedro Macati. At the town of Pasig, the view expanded into a vista of rolling hills.

On the evening of April 8, General Lawton and units of the Fourth Cavalry (dismounted), Fourteenth Infantry, and detachments from the Idaho, North Dakota, and Washington outfits boarded eight steamers and twenty barges for their journey up the Pasig River to the lake. Because of the winding, narrow channel and inexperienced river pilots, several boats ran aground. It was not until four o'clock the next morning that the flotilla reached the entrance of Laguna de Bay. They were joined by three gunboats under the command of Captain F. A. Grant.

At daybreak, the boats began their trip across the lake. A reporter aboard the Associated Press boat *Orient* wrote: "Before noon we lay in front of Santa Cruz. A stiff breeze swept the water as the men prepared to disembark and land on a stretch of beach that fronted a wide meadow. Because of the strong wind and high waves, many of the soldiers were forced to wade ashore in shoulder-deep water.

"When all the troops had reached the beach, we could see the long line of infantry form and begin their march inland. Sharp enemy fire opened up on the right of the soldiers, but after a half-hour it had ceased. Darkness came quickly, as it does in the tropics, and the brigade bivouacked for the night."

It was not quite daylight when General Lawton came ashore on the left of the American encampment. He walked along the front, speaking words of encouragement to the men who were about to go into battle.

The brigade's right flank was on the main road leading into the town from the south. As soon as the general was informed that the telegraph line from Santa Cruz had been cut, he gave the signal to advance.

The Americans met with little opposition until they reached the main bridge leading into the city. The rebels put up a terrific fight, but were no match for a wild bayonet charge by the Fourteenth Infantry.

In the meantime, Captain Gale's Fourth Cavalry had moved around to the north of the city and boxed in the enemy defenders. The Insurgents attempted to flee, but the only escape route open was across an empty field, where they came under punishing fire from the gunboats.

Captain Grant sent word to Lawton that the retreating rebels were moving toward the head of the lake, and the brigade set out in pursuit.

The Associated Press correspondent reported: "Our soldiers chased the Filipinos in the direction of Pagsanjan—a beautiful village nestled at the foot of the mountains on the north end of Laguna de Bay. At the edge of town, we marched down a broad avenue, paved with stone, and lined by coconut trees which gave us much welcome shade.

"We had only traveled about a mile on the picturesque boulevard, when the crack of Mausers was heard. The soldiers quickly deployed to the right and left of the road. We continued our advance, but met with no further resistance. Pagsanjan was taken without firing a shot.

"When our troops entered the village they found it deserted—with the exception of one old woman. However, there were many chickens and geese running about, and they made a tasty dinner for the hungry conquerors."

The brigade rested a couple of hours, and then moved forward along the Pagsanjan River toward the lake. A small Insurgent force made a stand, but was driven off. Six enemy launches and two barges were captured on the banks of the river. However, it was impossible to move the craft to the lake, since the Filipinos had placed obstructions in the water.

While waiting for the barriers to be removed, Major Weisenburger was directed to take a battalion and scout the area near Longos. When he reached the village, it was empty and foreboding. Major Fraine and two North Dakota companies moved out ahead to reconnoiter the trail between Longos and Paete.

The Dakota troops advanced cautiously. Thick jungle crowded both sides of the narrow path. After covering about a mile, a scout suddenly signaled back that a large number of rebels were seventy-five yards to the front—and behind strong entrenchments.

Major Fraine described the savage battle: "My sharpshooters were immediately brought up and deployed. At the same time, the enemy fired a heavy Mauser barrage into our lines. I sent a platoon from both companies through the jungle on either side of the trail. The left column hacked their way through the underbrush—while the platoon on the right dashed up a hill to flank the Insurgent position. The fighting was ferocious, and raged for more than two hours before a bayonet charge routed the Filipinos from their trenches. We entered Paete at six o'clock."

On April 15, General Elwell Otis sent word to Lawton to cancel the lake expedition and return to Manila "due to military necessity." The Twenty-second Infantry was also ordered to join the First Division at Manila.

General Lawton was directed to make preparations for a campaign into the countryside immediately east of the area now occupied by General MacArthur's troops. Up to this time, all of MacArthur's field operations had been conducted west of the Pinag de Candaba swamp. The marshes were impassable, except for a few roads that had been constructed through the rice fields.

The purpose of this new expedition was to drive the Insurgents from the territory between the Rio Grande de Pampanga River and the Bulacan Mountains.

Lawton's orders were to advance to Novaliches—then across the swamps and rice fields to San Jose—and on to Norzagaray, where a large rebel force had been reported.

At the same time, a Second Division brigade, under Colonel Owen Summers, would be marching from Bocaue to meet Lawton at Norzagaray—both commands then proceeding together to San Miguel.

The rest of MacArthur's division would head north from Malolos to Calumpit—then northeast to San Miguel. The final objective of this three-pronged movement was the capture of Aguinaldo's new capital at San Isidro.

On the evening of April 21, 1899, the First Division, plus two battalions of Third Infantry, assembled at the La Loma Church. Jacob Kreps wrote: "Each man was issued a hundred rounds of ammunition and rations for ten days. An additional hundred rounds was carried in carts drawn by carabao [water buffalo]—three carts for every two companies. In anticipation of bad roads, nothing was allowed on the wagons except rations and ammunition."

At five o'clock the following morning, Lawton's division moved out. The North Dakota troops led the march, and Captain Gale's Fourth Cavalry detachment brought up the rear.

A few miles south of Novaliches, the Americans encountered a strong enemy unit that occupied both sides of the road leading into the city. A fierce fire fight ensued, but the rebels were no match for the powerful division. Four North Dakota companies engaged the Insurgents and drove them across the Tuliahan River.

When Lawton entered Novaliches, he found the town deserted. The Filipinos had taken everything of value with them—including supplies of rice. The division bivouacked in native huts for the night.

Captain Kreps recalled: "The Twenty-second formed the outpost line to the northeast. During the afternoon, a group of rebels, entrenched on a hillside near the San Mateo road, opened fire on our pickets."

Map 7.2
Northern Luzon, Philippines, the Theater of Operations for the Twenty-second Infantry, 1899–1901

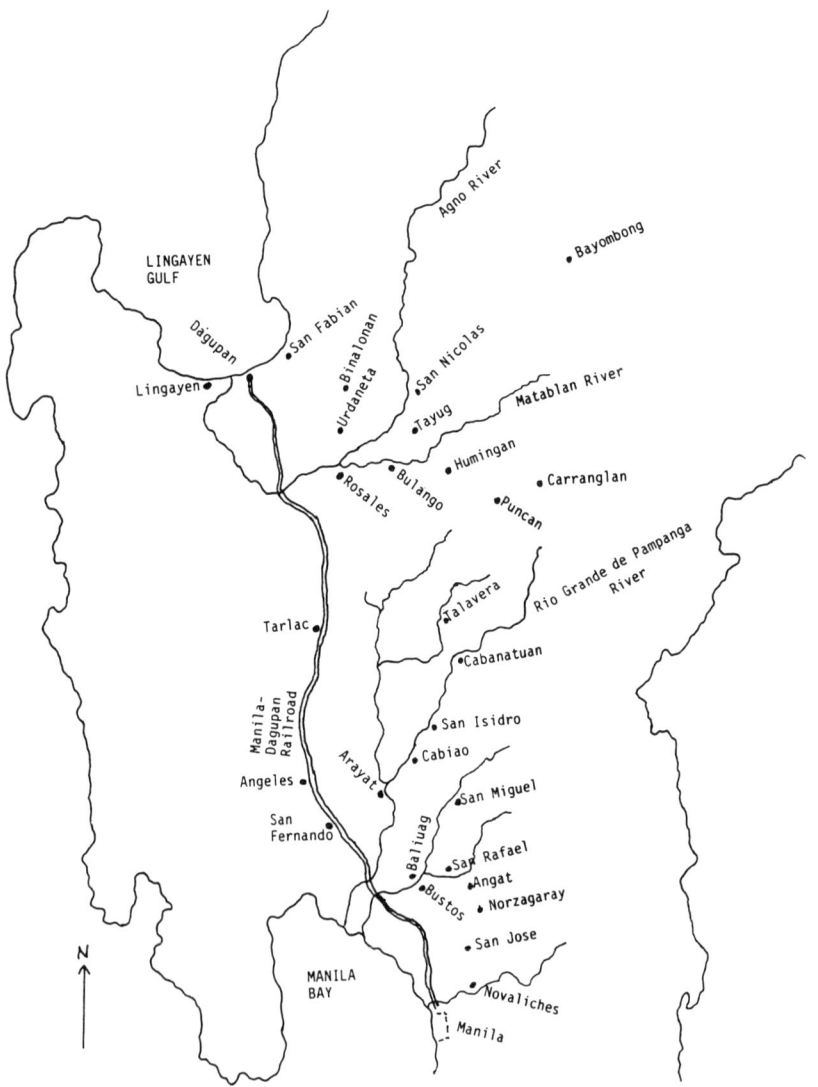

Their attack was only temporarily silenced. The enemy kept up an irritating, desultory fire throughout the night.

"At daybreak, our column advanced toward San Jose. The so-called road quickly became a mere footpath—winding its way across rice fields, through valleys, and over hills. All this while, the men and carabao were exposed to the sweltering rays of the tropical sun. The heat was intense. Hauling their heavy loads over the rugged trails, both man and animal soon became exhausted.

"Transportation was the most difficult part of this campaign. The rough roads, and oppressive temperatures, made it necessary to unhitch the carabaos at frequent intervals and lead them to water holes—letting the buffalo soak and wallow to recover their strength. But this wasn't the only inconvenience suffered during the march. A native guide intentionally led our column several miles in the wrong direction."

About three o'clock, the Twenty-second Regiment led the division across the Pasunkambor River—two miles south of San Jose. General Lawton bivouacked his troops for the night. However, the supply wagons were left four miles back—guarded by the Fourth Cavalry and a North Dakota detachment.

Jacob Kreps wrote on the wet pages of his notebook: "A tropical rainstorm lasted from nine until midnight—and added to the discomfort of the exhausted command. It was a fitful sleep—lying in pools of water and mud."

At eight o'clock in the morning, the Twenty-second Infantry marched into San Jose without opposition—but the supply wagons did not arrive until dark. Many of the carabao had died during the night, and the carts were hauled into camp by soldiers.

Captain Kreps continued: "On April 25, the advance resumed—with our regiment acting as rear guard. The movement of supplies worsened by the hour. Carabao kept dying—and men burdened with rifle, gun-belt, and blanket roll, yoked themselves to the wagons and pulled cart after cart up the long slopes."

While the soldiers of the First Division were trudging across hills and swamps, Colonel Summers' brigade closed in on Norzagaray and captured the city a few hours before General Lawton arrived.

The following day, in pouring rain, the combined brigades marched four miles to Angat—where they bivouacked in flooded rice fields and waited for the supply wagons to catch up.

However, another frustrating delay held back the American troops from continuing the chase of Aguinaldo. A Filipino peace commission had arrived in Manila. A new cabinet had been formed by Pedro Paterno, and he led a delegation of influential citizens for a meeting with General Elwell Otis.

Paterno's peace proposal demanded certain concessions—including a guarantee that the Insurgent army would be incorporated into the American military and not be forced to disband.

Once again, Otis refused to deal with the rebels. He was convinced that the revolt would soon collapse. Paterno angrily issued a proclamation blaming the Americans for refusing a truce and prolonging the war.

During the few days' respite from fighting, the Eighth Army Corps commander dispatched fifty pack mules and wagons, loaded with rations and ammunition for the troops at Angat.

The delay also gave American intelligence officers an opportunity to question captured Insurgents. A rebel officer revealed that the Filipino defenders of Novaliches and San Jose did not obey orders from Aguinaldo, but acted independently. They had been brainwashed into believing that they would be tortured or killed if they surrendered.

At daybreak on April 29, Lawton's division proceeded down the south bank of the Bagbag River toward San Rafael. Colonel Summers' brigade headed along the north bank. About noon, Colonel Treumann's North Dakota detachment was ambushed by about four hundred Insurgents. After a short, fierce battle, the enemy force withdrew downstream.

The history of the Twenty-second Infantry scouts had been legendary since the early days on the western frontier. William H. Young was no exception. He continually dressed like a native Filipino.

General Lawton had often noticed Young walking far in front of the advance guard and was afraid that the scout might be shot by his own men. Lawton intended to reprimand Young and send him to the rear. However, the general changed his mind, and asked the scout to sneak into San Rafael and bring back a native for interrogation.

Bill Young eagerly accepted the assignment and quickly disappeared into the brush. About five minutes later, a volley of shots was heard. At first, Lawton was concerned that he had sent the scout to his death, but then Young was suddenly spotted walking calmly out of the jungle. He strolled nonchalantly back to division headquarters—carrying an enemy rifle, haversack, and ammunition belt—all soaked with blood.

Young reported to the general that he had run into a rebel outpost of eight men. He killed one of the Insurgents and drove off the others.

Lawton was more than impressed. He placed Bill Young in charge of a detachment of twenty-five volunteer scouts, and they soon became an integral part of the division.

On April 30, two companies of the Twenty-second were sent to meet the pack mules and escort the supply train to Angat. The rations and ammunition were quickly distributed, and the Americans continued their march to San Rafael.

Young and his men checked the jungle ahead. About two miles from the village they dispersed as skirmishers. Taking advantage of trees and heavy brush, the scouts silently approached their objective. Upon reaching a clearing in front of the village, they rushed the town—firing weapons in all directions, and yelling at the top of their lungs. Pandemonium ran rampant—it sounded to the rebels like the entire United States Army was attacking San Rafael.

The Insurgents dropped their rifles and fled—the scouts chasing them through the streets. Bill Young broke into the town's church and dashed to the belfry. He rang the bell as a signal that all was clear, and it was now safe for more than a thousand American soldiers to enter the village.

The following morning, both commands continued their advance down the Bagbag River. Summers' column headed toward Baliuag, on the north bank—while Lawton approached Bustos on the south shore.

About two miles out from San Rafael, Summers' brigade came upon a large group of refugees composed mainly of women and children. However, many wounded soldiers were noticed being carried on litters. They were heading north in the direction of San Miguel.

Summers ordered his column to halt and sent a detachment forward with a flag of truce, but when his men came within five hundred yards of the Filipinos, the rebel troops opened fire. The flag detail scurried safely back to their own lines. Summers let the refugees and wounded continue their journey unmolested.

Bill Young's scouts chopped their way through the jungle, staying about a mile ahead of Lawton's division. Suddenly, without warning, the pickets were ambushed by a concealed enemy force near the outskirts of Bustos.

The sound of heavy gunfire quickly brought the Twenty-second Infantry to the rescue. The regiment deployed as they dashed through the woods—and, screaming war-whoops like a tribe of Sioux Indians, the soldiers chased the Insurgents back behind formidable stone barricades that surrounded the city.

While the rebels were still in a state of shock from the Twenty-second Regiment's rampage, Lawton sent two battalions to the right flank. As soon as his brigades were in position, the signal was given for a simultaneous frontal and flank assault on the town.

It was a picture-perfect attack, as the American troops charged the masonry breastworks—driving the confused enemy from the city. Within an hour, Bustos was captured, and a large number of Filipinos taken prisoner.

On the other side of the river, Colonel Summers and his brigade had butted up against a strong Insurgent defense at Baliuag. Lawton directed his scout detachment to sneak across the river and rush the town from the rear.

Young and his men crossed the stream unseen and attacked the rebels from behind. The Filipinos were now completely surrounded, and their defenses crumbled under the ruthless pressure from all sides. The scouts broke through the door of the city's cathedral, and Bill Young rang the bells to announce the victory.

Captain Kreps commented on the day's action: "The natives of Bustos and Baliuag—like those of other towns we had captured—fled their homes when they heard that we were approaching. The citizens had been propagandized by Aguinaldo into fearing the Americans. However, within a short time after our occupation of Baliuag, the natives began to sneak back into town. By nightfall, practically the entire population had returned. They had heard from civilians, of other communities we had passed through, that our troops treated the people with courtesy and respect.

"An enormous quantity of rice, that had been stored by the rebels, was discovered in the city. Thousands of bushels were distributed to the famished populace. Many people—in a frenzy of hunger—groveled in the storehouse, cramming their mouths with the raw grain. This rice had been confiscated by the Insurgents to feed their army—leaving the women and children to die from starvation."

Intelligence reports indicated that there were numerous rebel grain and supply depots between Baliuag and San Miguel. General Lawton called upon his scouts for a different kind of mission. Young and his men received their orders: "To search the countryside for the purpose of locating and destroying all warehouses and caches of Insurgent sustenance and other supplies. Careful records of stores destroyed should be kept, and reports of progress should be sent at every practical opportunity. The scouts will carry no rations, but live off the land."

Within two days, Bill Young and his detachment had located forty storehouses of rice. However, the buildings were built of stone with iron roofs. They could not be burned without damaging the homes of nearby villagers.

Colonel Summers was directed to conduct an examination of the depots. He reported that they contained at least 150,000 bushels of rice and sixty-five tons of sugar. Rather than destroy such a large amount of food, it was distributed to local families—and also used to supplement the rations issued to the soldiers.

On May 7, the city of Baliuag held an election. Jacob Kreps recorded the event: "Señor Francisco Guerrero was selected as mayor—the first native to hold office in the Philippines under the jurisdiction of the United States. This liberal policy of self-government was eagerly welcomed by the people—and oaths of allegiance were freely taken. Later it was discovered that even greater freedom was exercised in violating these sacred promises.

"The first mayor of Baliuag came in daily contact with American officers—and all information gathered by him was promptly reported to Aguinaldo. When the mayor's treachery was found out, he was tried, convicted, and sentenced to a long term of imprisonment."

On May 13, General Lawton received a message from Eighth Army Corps Headquarters, authorizing him to pay thirty dollars (Mexican) for each serviceable rifle delivered over to his command by any Insurgent. Lawton published the order in Spanish and Tagalog (Filipino), and it was widely disseminated. Every effort was also made to circulate the directive in rebel-controlled areas.

The following morning, the First Division began its march toward San Miguel. Bill Young and his men scouted ahead. Captain Birkhimer, with two Oregon companies, stuck close to the pickets—while Major Eastwick and the rest of the Oregon battalion remained a short distance behind.

When the scouts reached the village of San Ildefonso, they were suddenly surprised by a large band of Insurgents. Birkhimer reached the scene of action in minutes and found Young's troops heavily engaged on the right. The Oregon captain rapidly deployed his companies along the enemy front and sent the scouts on a wide detour.

Young's detachment took their position on a knoll that commanded the rebel left flank. As soon as Eastwick arrived, the Americans charged the Filipino positions—routing the enemy north from the town.

Captain Birkhimer stated: "After the engagement, an officer of Aguinaldo's army approached our lines under a flag of truce. He requested permission for General Pilar to be granted safe passage to Manila for another attempt at a negotiated settlement of the war. General Elwell Otis was notified—but believed that this was just another scheme to delay MacArthur's offensive until the start of the rainy season. However, Otis did agree to make arrangements for Pilar to travel to Manila. In the meantime, we were to continue pressing the rebels."

While the First Division and Colonel Summers' brigade advanced toward San Miguel, Bill Young and ten of his scouts recklessly put a couple of thousand yards between themselves and the advance guard. This time, however, the Filipinos were ready and waiting for them.

The scouts had no sooner reached the outskirts of town when they were attacked by an enemy skirmish line. The Insurgents were hidden behind dikes—about two hundred yards distant. The rebel right flank was concealed in bamboo thickets along the riverbank—and the left was dug in on a hill protected by a steep ravine.

Young quickly realized that neither flank could be turned. His detachment was trapped. If his men stayed in one place or tried to retreat, they would still be picked off—one by one.

The chief scout decided that, if he was going to die, he might as well do it with style. Whooping and hollering, the scouts charged the center of the enemy front. Believing that the American army was only moments away, the Insurgents took off running toward the river.

The scouts continued their pursuit of the rebels as the Filipinos attempted to scramble across the stream, but William Young's luck was about to run out. He was fatally wounded while urging his men onward.

Minutes later, the Oregon, Minnesota, and Third Infantry battalions arrived. By evening, San Miguel was in American hands. General Lawton recommended all of the scouts for the Medal of Honor.

General MacArthur had originally been ordered to join Lawton and Summers at San Miguel, but he was redirected to meet them at Arayat.

Captain Kreps commented: "With the exception of Baliuag, this was the most important city occupied so far by the expedition. There were many elegant homes and other evidences of a wealthy community. As soon as San Miguel was captured, the inhabitants began to return from the hills where they had taken refuge.

"There were large numbers of Chinese in the more populated towns. They constituted the merchant class and owned many small shops. The Chinese had been assessed exorbitantly high war taxes by the Insurgent officials—in lieu of which they were to receive protection from the Filipino soldiers. However, many of the Orientals were still ruthlessly slaughtered."

On the morning of May 17, 1899, the American troops continued their advance to San Isidro. The Twenty-second Infantry, now commanded by Colonel J. W. French, was deployed to the left of the road. The North Dakota and Oregon battalions moved ahead on the right.

When Lawton's scouts were within two thousand yards of the city, the rebels opened fire, but by the time Colonel French and his troops arrived, there was only a small rear guard detachment to oppose the Americans. Aguinaldo, with a large part of his army, had fled into the jungle and hills near Naguilian.

The following afternoon, two battalions of the Twenty-second, along with the North Dakota volunteers, proceeded down the Rio Grande de Pampanga. Captain Kreps described the march: "About two o'clock we encountered a band of Insurgents at the village of San Fernando. We deployed under fire and forced the enemy across the river. However, due to the depth of the water, we were unable to follow them. The rebels took defensive positions on the opposite riverbank. An attempt was made to dislodge the Filipinos with artillery. But the range was short—less than two hundred yards—and many of the shells exploded too soon, endangering our own men with flying shrapnel.

"During the night, the enemy kept up an annoying fire, but by daylight only a few Filipinos remained—the others having disappeared into the jungle. We moved out, and, after a short skirmish, occupied Cabiao. General Lawton soon joined us with the rest of the division, and the next morning we marched on Arayat."

Captain Ballance and his Twenty-second Infantry battalion led the attack. The scouts deployed ahead, expecting at any moment to be fired upon. However, there was not one crack from a Mauser, whiz of a bullet, or a single enemy soldier in sight. The rebels had already left for the hill country to join Aguinaldo.

Many residents were still in Arayat, and others kept returning throughout the day. General MacArthur arrived about noon, and the combined divisions bivouacked for the night.

Jacob Kreps narrated: "On May 23, while we were moving downriver toward Candaba, heavy firing was heard in the direction of San Miguel. Ballance's battalion was sent to investigate, but the swamps prevented his troops from getting close enough to discover the cause.

"We later learned that the Third Infantry, under Captain Hannay, had been ambushed four times on their march from San Miguel to Baliuag. The journey, covering only fourteen miles, took fifteen hours to complete. The Insurgent hit-and-run forces were driven off with heavy losses, but these sneak attacks were a dangerous portend of things to come."

Chapter Eight

THE CAMPAIGN SOUTH OF MANILA

Emilio Aguinaldo soon realized that it was foolhardy for his untrained and poorly equipped troops to continue fighting pitched battles against professional soldiers. He wisely changed his strategy and adopted guerrilla warfare tactics. However, veteran units, such as the Seventy-third Regiment, were kept intact for direct confrontations with American forces.

A captured Insurgent directive detailed the crafty rebel leader's plans: "Officers will give instructions to their soldiers—making them understand their duties as defenders of the country—and inflicting upon them disciplinary punishment when necessary.

"In order that the enemy may not be able to distinguish our soldiers when, for instance, an ambush is being prepared, have them dress as country people—not permitting anyone, including officers, to wear uniforms.

"All troop commanders shall observe prudence—while, at the same time, employing every artifice to defeat the enemy."

On the evening of May 23, 1899, General Elwell Otis terminated the northern expedition. The Twenty-second Infantry Regiment was assigned to MacArthur's division. Colonel French's troops were split up and garrisoned at Candaba, San Luis, and San Fernando.

General Lawton and the rest of the First Division were ordered to San Pedro Macati to prepare for a campaign against Paranaque.

Captain Kreps and Company M, stationed at San Luis, were engaged in constant skirmishes with small rebel units. The enemy would strike quickly and unexpectedly from concealed locations—fleeing before a counterattack could be made. Kreps described the frustrations of fighting a guerrilla war: "Our forces were greatly annoyed by their inability to locate bands of harassing Insurgents. Outposts and scouting parties, investigating shots fired at them, would only find 'peaceful natives' working in the fields.

"Whenever a large body of American troops passed through a certain area—only amicable Filipinos were to be seen. However, small army detachments, marching along the same path, were constantly attacked.

"The belief prevailed that the Insurgent chieftains had authorized a type of warfare contrary to the rules of civilized nations. Occasionally a native was caught wearing a rebel uniform under his ordinary clothes. And many American officers began to take for granted that every Filipino was their enemy.

"The rebels were able to appear and disappear as they wished. At their own discretion they would attack as soldiers, and an hour later were within American lines as peace loving farmers. The peculiarity of this war has placed in the hands of the Insurgent leaders a perfect system of espionage—which often upset our carefully laid plans.

"Almost every village—captured or not—furnished Aguinaldo's soldiers with food and supplies. The Eighth Army Corps began to believe that they were fighting the entire population of the Philippines.

"At the same time, however, our troops were under strict orders to protect peaceful citizens. So, despite the predicament, officers and men fought and worked with steadfast fidelity—each man realizing that the issue of the campaign depended on his individual efforts.

"Day after scorching day, every soldier was armed, alert, and exposed to the roasting sun—which was almost as killing, and often harder to bear, than the enemy Mausers. Devotion and duty increased with adversity. The corps was ready and eager to confront the rebels as occasion demanded."

The Third Battalion of the Twenty-second Regiment was bivouacked at San Fernando to guard the railroad. A long row of Insurgent trenches stretched across the northern front of the battalion's line. Practically every night, the Filipinos kept up a constant barrage of rifle fire—and often launched nuisance raids against the American defenses. Company H was kept busy pushing an armored railroad car—by hand—a mile to the front to repulse enemy attacks.

After Aguinaldo had retreated into the hills, General Elwell Otis decided to concentrate his efforts on the countryside south of Manila. At five o'clock on the morning of June 10, General Lawton and his division departed San Pedro Macati—the line of march taking the troops across the Guadalupe ridge.

The object of this campaign was to clear the rebels from the territory between the lake and Manila Bay. The terrain was rugged—cut by gulches and overgrown with tall grass and chaparral. A newspaper correspondent described the night in camp before the march: "The men slept without tents, even though rain poured down heavily for an hour. But the soldiers only laughed—for in the gentle air of these favored isles, rain, however much it dampens the body, seldom chills. Then again, the lust for war was in our blood—and we knew that tommorrow would show us the terrible beauty of skilled and legal murder!"

Lawton's division was composed of two brigades commanded by Generals Ovenshine and Wheaton. Ovenshine's brigade consisted of the Twelfth, Thirteenth, and Fourteenth Infantry Regiments. Wheaton's battalions included the Ninth and Twenty-first Infantries, the Colorado volunteers, and batteries from the First and Sixth Artillery units.

The division moved silently along the Pasig River. When they reached the Guadalupe ridge, the brigades separated. Ovenshine's troops headed southwest toward Paranaque and Manila Bay—while Wheaton and General Lawton moved down the west shore of Laguna de Bay. Both brigades were to meet at Paranaque.

About seven o'clock, Insurgents entrenched on a hilltop near the lake stood up in their rifle pits and fired down upon the advancing Colorado detachment. The men dove for cover, but Lieutenant Colonel Moses rallied his soldiers and charged up the slope. The rebels were routed from their position; however, Moses was wounded as he jumped into an enemy trench.

Lawton, dressed in white and riding a black horse, made a perfect target for the Filipino sharpshooters. Mauser bullets splattered the ground on all sides of the general, but he was untouched.

Along the lake shore, the hot sun was overpowering. The Americans discarded their blanket rolls and haversacks, and stripped to the waist. Canteens were soon empty, and there was no source of fresh water to replenish the supply. A tortuous thirst began to preoccupy the minds of the soldiers. The troops were exhausted from the heat, and many dropped out of column because of sunstroke.

About three o'clock, the brigade turned west toward Las Pinas—a

Map 8.1
The Campaign Area South of Manila

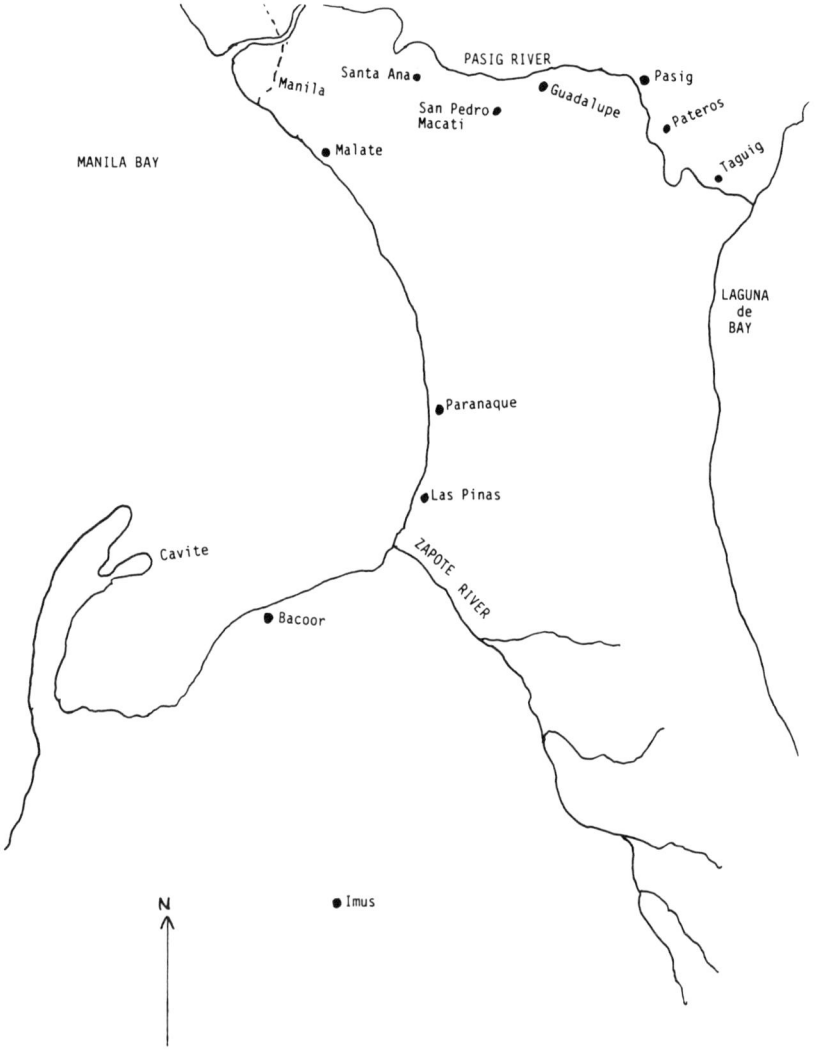

few miles below Paranaque. However, unknown to Generals Wheaton and Lawton, their fatigued troops had been constantly stalked by the rebels. Near Las Pinas, the brigade was ambushed by a large force of Insurgents who had concealed themselves in a bamboo grove. Before the Americans could form a skirmish line, another enemy detachment struck from the rear. The brigade had its hands full, but finally succeeded in driving off the Filipinos.

Wheaton's thirsty and battle-weary soldiers continued their advance, but rebel snipers, hiding in trees, waited until the last battalion had passed and then shot stragglers as the men attempted to keep up with the column.

Two of Admiral Dewey's warships, the U.S.S. *Monadnock* and U.S.S. *Helena,* stood offshore and shelled Paranaque and Las Pinas throughout the day.

About evening, a violent thunderstorm ripped across the bay, forcing General Wheaton to bivouac his troops until morning. Many "supposedly lost" soldiers wandered into camp during the night.

At daybreak, General Lawton led the brigade into Las Pinas. The march was unopposed. Leaving a small detachment in the city, Wheaton headed for Paranaque—entering the town at seven o'clock.

Although the Insurgents had vacated Paranaque, the women and children remained in their homes. Many houses were damaged by the fleet bombardment, and white flags flew from nearly every building.

Meanwhile, General Ovenshine's brigade had crossed the Guadalupe ridge and advanced through the tall grass until they came to the edge of the rice fields. The rebels had hidden behind the dikes and anxiously waited until the approaching battalions were within point-blank range—then pulled the triggers on their Mausers.

Fortunately for the Americans, the nervous Filipinos fired wildly and erratically. The Thirteenth and Fourteenth Regiments formed a skirmish line, and Captain Scott's Sixth Artillery was called up.

Shrapnel from exploding shells decimated the enemy defenses, and Ovenshine ordered his brigade to move forward. However, progress across the swampy rice fields was difficult. The Insurgents, entrenched along the front and on the flanks, had little trouble picking off the slow-moving Americans. The Fourteenth Infantry was stalled in mud two feet deep. Only by marching single file—each soldier trodding in the footsteps of the man in front of him—were the troops able to make any headway.

Scouts from the Ninth and Twenty-first Regiments finally located a dry crossing through the fields. The beleaguered brigade quickly flanked the enemy positions, and a savage bayonet charge sent the Filipinos fleeing into the woods. Ovenshine's battalions entered Paranaque a few hours after Wheaton had arrived.

The following morning, June 13, General Lawton, with two companies of Twenty-first Infantry, scouted southwest in the direction of Bacoor. About a mile from the city, the detachment was ambushed by a large band of rebels. The enemy force was overpowering, and Lawton withdrew to await reinforcements. Gunboats, in the bay, were given coordinates for naval gunfire support. Additional troops and artillery were rapidly deployed, and one of the fiercest battles of the war began.

The American attack was centered on the bridge across the Zapote River. One company of Fourteenth Infantry and an artillery battery advanced cautiously along the road to Bacoor. The rest of the regiment moved forward to the right and left of the trail.

The Insurgents had dug deep trenches along the Bacoor side of the river. The wooden bridge had been partially burned to prevent the Americans from crossing the stream.

Captain Kenley brought his artillery battery up to the bridge and blasted the rebel rifle pits on the other side of the river, but these trenches were excellently constructed. The shells had little, if any, effect—even though Kenley's guns were only thirty-five yards from the enemy positions.

A rifle duel quickly developed. However, from this short range, Lawton's sharpshooters clearly had the upper hand. After a half-hour of punishment, the Filipinos deserted their trenches. The American troops ran along the edge of the river—firing at the fleeing rebels. The Fourteenth Infantry swam the river and occupied the rifle pits. Insurgent losses were heavy—more than fifty bodies were counted near the Bacoor side of the bridge.

However, the fighting was far from over—a second row of breastworks were less than a mile away. Fresh soldiers were rushed in to support the Fourteenth Infantry's assault.

Under the protection of Admiral Dewey's fleet, a company of marines was landed behind the enemy rear. At the same time, units of the Ninth and Twelfth Regiments crossed the river at a sandbar and joined the marines in back of the rebel left flank.

In the meantime, the Twenty-first Regiment repaired the bridge and stormed over the rickety structure—driving the Filipinos from their last line of defense. Sixty Insurgents were found dead in the trenches—most of them shot through the head. Several five-inch smooth bore guns were also discovered, along with ammunition marked "United States Navy."

The rebel rear guard put up a vigorous defense, while the rest of Aguinaldo's troops escaped into a thick jungle of bamboo groves. General Wheaton deployed his battalions and rushed the woods. The battle was vicious—an Insurgent behind every bush and snipers in the trees.

General Lawton continually placed himself in harm's way—riding his black stallion back and forth across the front line. He made a perfect target with the sun's rays glistening off his white pith helmet. Although the general's bravery was an inspiration to his men, it also was a reflection on the poor marksmanship of the Filipinos.

The enemy withdrew about five miles inland to a line of defenses around the town of Imus—where they could regroup and still be out of naval gun range.

Early the next morning, Lawton and a troop of Fourth Cavalry carefully reconnoitered along the shore of Manila Bay and marched into Bacoor unopposed. The town had been battered by Dewey's fleet. Civilians fled to the hills during the bombardment and watched the warships pulverize their homes. Practically every building, including a large church, was reduced to rubble.

Several hundred refugees, with nothing left to return to, crowded across the American lines. The roads were jammed with natives—carrying possessions in baskets on their heads and driving livestock in front of them. Lawton's soldiers shared their canned beef rations with the refugees, and rice was also distributed to the populace.

On June 18, General Wheaton's brigade was ordered to Imus, but no enemy troops were encountered as the brigade entered and searched the deserted city.

The surrounding countryside, however, had not been scouted. A battalion of Fourth Infantry and Major John Bubb's gun battery were sent out to reconnoiter south of town.

The detachment had only advanced a mile when they were suddenly attacked by a large group of Insurgents. The sound of heavy gunfire was heard in Imus. Wheaton immediately rushed two infantry battalions and an artillery unit to the scene of action. The artillery quickly flanked the rebels and opened fire with devastating effect. The Filipinos broke ranks and fled in the direction of Dasmarinas.

General Wheaton regrouped his regiments and pursued the enemy. After several fierce clashes, the Insurgents scattered into the jungle.

The land area for several miles south of Manila was now in American hands—but north of the capital, it was a different story. Aguinaldo had moved the seat of his revolutionary government to Tarlac—eighty miles north of Manila. The Insurgent leader still controlled more than half the island of Luzon.

Jacob Kreps described the frustration of trying to fight a war during the Philippine rainy season: "The companies at Candaba were constantly engaged in reconnaissance. Daily thunderstorms soon turned the rice fields into lakes, and scouting parties were compelled to trudge through waist-high water.

"On August 9, the Third Battalion, under Major J. A. Baldwin, participated in General MacArthur's advance from San Fernando. The battle line formed before daylight—fronting the enemy earthworks on the north side of town. The engagement began with an artillery barrage directed at rebel strong points. Although they were taken by surprise, the Insurgents put up a spirited defense. Within a half-hour, however, enemy fire slackened and our brigades moved forward.

"The march was extremely difficult. Incessant tropical rains had changed the ground to a muddy bog of tangled grass. As our troops plodded ahead, they came under ragged fire from the retreating Filipinos. The enemy trenches had been abandoned, but were filled with dead and wounded.

"Baldwin's battalion sloshed through a labyrinth of tall sugar cane. Physical resources were taxed to the utmost. The intense heat and lack of air in the cane fields were intolerable. It took more than six hours to cover seven miles—and forty soldiers collapsed from exhaustion. One man, carried from the field, died without regaining consciousness."

On October 12, 1899, the First and Third Battalions of the Twenty-second Infantry Regiment received orders to join General Samuel Young's brigade at Arayat. The long-awaited campaign against Aguinaldo's army in northern Luzon was about to begin.

Chapter Nine

THE MARCH TO LINGAYEN GULF

For nearly a year, the Eighth Army Corps had been fighting a losing battle trying to chase the Insurgents from the valley north of Manila. The rebels continued to control the Manila-Dagupan Railroad from Angeles to the Lingayen Gulf.

General Elwell Otis was determined to capture the entire length of the railroad with a force strong enough to hold the tracks permanently. He was certain that once the railroad was in American hands—and ocean ports blockaded—Aguinaldo's grip on Luzon would be broken. The rebel leader would no longer be able to equip his army with imported guns and ammunition. He would be forced to surrender when his current supplies were exhausted. Otis theorized that, once the valley was occupied by the United States Army, the natives would most likely return to their homes and farms.

Meanwhile, Aguinaldo had been busy assembling an imposing army of 25,000 men—recruited from the many islands of the Philippines. Aguinaldo believed that by using hit-and-run tactics, from bases in mountain hideaways, he would be able to prolong the war indefinitely.

Captain Kreps stated: "The plan of this campaign was to hold the Insurgents in their present positions while the American Army closed the northern and eastern escape routes to the mountains—then to capture or scatter the rebels—take possession of the railroad—and pursue the enemy's retreating detachments.

"Three columns were to be used in executing the maneuver. General

MacArthur's division was to clear the Insurgents from the railroad all the way to Dagupan on the Lingayen Gulf.

"General Wheaton's regiments were to travel by sea and make an amphibious landing at San Fabian. Wheaton would then swing east and south—closing all roads leading into the mountains.

"Sam Young's brigade drew the most difficult assignment. His column was ordered north from Arayat—through Cabanatuan, and then on to San Nicolas. All three columns were to meet north of Tarlac—hopefully sealing off the rebels in a giant trap."

In addition to two battalions of Twenty-second Infantry, General Young's force included the Twenty-fourth and Thirty-fourth Regiments, two battalions of the Thirty-seventh Infantry, and three troops of cavalry. The forward scouting units consisted of an American detachment under Captain Lowe and two companies of Macabebe scouts. The Macabebes were Filipino natives who joined the Eighth Army Corps after the fall of Manila.

Jacob Kreps described the beginning of the offensive: "General Young began his advance on the evening of October 17, 1899. Captain Ballance's battalion crossed the Rio Grande de Pampanga at dark and proceeded up the river. Their orders were to clear the way for the main column which was to follow at daybreak.

"The enemy was reported strongly entrenched at Maglibutad. Lowe's scouts were directed to move along the right bank of the river, while the Macabebes reconnoitered the left side. Shortly before dawn, the scouts located the rebel trenches. However, in the darkness, the Macabebes failed to reach their assigned position. Ballance could not afford to wait on the native scouts and risk losing the element of surprise. The First Battalion immediately launched a direct assault along the Insurgent front. The enemy resisted fiercely, but was unable to halt the surge of the American line. A screaming bayonet charge finally drove the rebels from the breastworks, and they fled toward Cabiao—leaving more than a hundred dead and wounded comrades in the rifle pits."

Ballance's men dashed in pursuit of the Filipinos—meeting only weak opposition from the Insurgent rear guard. The enemy retreated in mass confusion along both sides of the river—firing indiscriminately in their rush to escape.

Captain Kreps continued: "Due to the bedlam, the rebels on the right bank of the river began shooting at their own men on the other side of the stream. Pandemonium quickly replaced reason as the Filipinos shot at each other in desperation. Our scouts added to the frenzy by unleashing a savage rifle barrage. The enemy fell back in disarray—dazed, and demoralized."

At daylight, General Sam Young's brigade moved out, with Ballance's battalion acting as the advance guard. Major Baldwin and the Third Battalion were instructed to remain at Arayat to guard the town and escort supply wagons to the front.

Near San Isidro, Lowe's scouts stumbled upon a company of Insurgents who were busily engaged in tearing down a rope bridge that traversed a deep part of the river. A rapid fire attack sent the rebels scurrying into the woods. The scouts rushed the span and crossed hand-over-hand, holding on to cables that had not yet been cut. Several soldiers were shot and splashed into the water, while others lost their grip on the swaying lines.

Half of Lowe's detachment managed to reach the other side and formed a protective ring around the bridge. Private Charles Pierce was severely wounded, but refused medical attention and continued firing his rifle at the unseen enemy. Pierce was awarded the Medal of Honor for gallantry in action.

The advance guard arrived on the run, and deployed in the mud and water along the riverbank. Jacob Kreps reported: "The enemy retreated to a natural barricade formed by trees and a thick bamboo grove. In front of the barrier was an open area, averaging forty yards in width. The Insurgents, keeping well concealed, massed behind the thicket. Upon reaching the open space, the battalion suddenly received heavy fire at close range. Without hesitation, Captain Ballance and his troops charged the woods, driving the rebels out.

"Had the distance been greater, or the marksmanship of the Filipinos more accurate, this position could not have been taken without suffering greater casualties. The ambuscade was well planned—but our prompt assault completely unnerved the Insurgents, and they fled in the direction of San Isidro."

The First Battalion resumed its march. One company was sent along the river path, and the rest of the battalion proceeded on the main road to San Isidro.

Captain Ballance expected heavy opposition as he neared the city and requested reinforcements. General Young promptly dispatched three troops of dismounted cavalry and six guns to the front. The scouts located the enemy earthworks about a mile south of town. Ballance formed his skirmish lines on both sides of the road. The battalion plodded laboriously through a series of submerged rice fields until they reached the city's outer defenses. Then with a yell, reminiscent of their days on the western frontier, Ballance and his men rushed the rebel trenches. The Insurgents fled in disorder and were chased several miles beyond the city limits.

In the meantime, Major Baldwin's Third Battalion was kept continually busy. The river was scouted daily, and the important ferry at Arayat was kept manned and guarded. Captain Kreps described the difficulties encountered in keeping the supply lines open: "The great quantity of stores passing through the town necessitated strong outposts. The job of forwarding rations and ammunition across the river on the flat-bottomed boat was an arduous task. Due to intermittent rains, the stream rose and fell rapidly. At high water, the wooden, corduroyed landing piers were submerged. And when the water receded, the wharves had to be dug out from under several inches of mud and slush.

"At one time, when the river was a raging torrent, a passing barge cut the main rope that guided the ferry from one shore to the other. Major Baldwin and his men worked constantly in the water for thirty-six hours to repair the break."

General Young bivouacked his brigade at San Isidro until the early morning of October 27. At four o'clock the advance was resumed. Captain Ballance's battalion and Lowe's scouts led the march. They were reinforced by a dismounted cavalry troop and six field pieces.

When the First Battalion reached the Tombo River crossing, they discovered that the Insurgents had destroyed the bridge and constructed breastworks on the other side. Captain Ballance instructed the artillery to wait for the main column and then had his infantry build bamboo rafts. In the early morning darkness, the soldiers floated silently across the water and routed the surprised rebels.

After reconnoitering ahead another mile, Captain Lowe's scouts spotted a detachment of Aguinaldo's elite Seventy-third Regiment. They were hurrying toward the Rio Grande de Pampanga to attack one of Captain Grant's river gunboats. The enemy soldiers made a beautiful target—dressed in their gaudy Spanish-made uniforms—red trousers, white straw hats, and shirts of various colors. Company F was ordered to attack and made short work of the arrogant outfit.

The scouts pushed on—there was no such thing as a "rest-break."

After a couple of hours of forced march, Lowe and his men encountered a rebel outpost near the Taboatin River. After carefully scouting the area, Captain Lowe stated: "Reconnaissance revealed that the bridge at this site had been completely destroyed. The river was unfordable due to recent torrential rains, and the banks on either side were very steep. The Insurgents occupied a line of trenches for eight hundred yards along the opposite shore."

The scouts and Company A were sent on a wide detour to the right. They crossed the river two miles above the entrenchments—intending to swing around the rebel defenses.

In the meantime, the Macabebes and Company K were ordered forward. The soldiers crawled quietly through tall brush and grass until they were almost to the water's edge. Artillery was moved up—guns were loaded and range calibrated. Captain Ballance wrote: "These preparations were made so secretly that the Filipinos were in complete ignorance of our movements. We watched the enemy sentinels on the other side of the river. They were busy chattering among themselves—entirely oblivious as to what was going on about them. At my signal, our infantry and artillery opened fire with a savage barrage. However, we were unable to drive the Insurgents from their trenches.

"I suddenly learned that, due to unforeseen difficulties, the scouts and Company A had not reached their objective. I immediately sent two more companies up river with instructions to cross a half-mile above the rifle pits and attack the enemy flank."

Wading, swimming, and floating on bamboo rafts, the Americans succeeded in fording the stream. The Insurgents discovered the assault—but too late. After firing a few volleys at the men in the water, the rebels abandoned their positions and escaped into the jungle. The remainder of the First Battalion crossed the river on rafts, and that evening the American forces occupied Santa Rosa.

Captain Ballance and his advance guard captured Cabanatuan on October 30, and General Young arrived with the rest of the brigade on the following day. However, in order to continue their march north, it was again necessary for the troops to cross the Rio Grande de Pampanga. Ballance stated: "The river was at flood stage and running very fast. A temporary ferry was built to transport the companies across—but it was perilous work. One man was drowned, and four others barely rescued from the strong current by the heroic efforts of their comrades."

On November 10, Major Baldwin's battalion was relieved of supply escort duty and ordered to Cabanatuan. Jacob Kreps wrote: "Heavy rains had turned the ground into a mass of sticky mud. After marching two days—from daylight until dark—the battalion had only covered twelve miles. Over much of the journey, ammunition and ration wagons were pulled by soldiers. We finally arrived at Cabanatuan on November 15."

Sam Young had a tremendous amount of confidence in Captain Ballance. As soon as the general received word that Major Baldwin was on his way from Arayat, Young directed Ballance to head north through Talavera, San Jose, and Humingan. The First Battalion's orders were to join General Wheaton's column, which had landed at San Fabian on November 7 and was moving south.

The road beyond Cabanatuan was nothing but a trough of mud. Troops ran ahead of the column—cutting brush, grass, bamboo—anything to make a solid foundation for men and wagons to travel over. For several miles, the carabao pulled only empty carts—soldiers carried supplies on their backs until the battalion reached firmer ground.

The First Battalion occupied San Jose on the 12th and Humingan on the 13th. Captain Ballance narrated: "By this time, the shoes and clothing of the men were in deplorable condition. The number of soldiers marching barefooted increased daily. Upon reaching San Jose, we received orders to leave all 'impediments' behind. Therefore, we left town carrying nothing but our rifles, a hundred rounds of ammunition per man, one full day's rations, and three emergency rations. Two miles out from San Jose, we passed a cavalry troop which had left a day earlier. They were hopelessly stuck in the mud.

"I stationed one company to hold Humingan. The rest of the battalion was cut loose from the brigade—with urgent orders to proceed as fast as possible to Rosales, and attack a strong Insurgent force near Urdaneta. The enemy army was reported to be at least five thousand strong.

"My instructions were to take two pieces of artillery and attempt to sneak behind the rebel defenses. Moving cautiously—unimpeded by wagon trains—we outflanked an enemy detachment at Bulango and chased the Insurgents across the Matablan River. The Filipinos destroyed the bridge—taking up the flooring and cutting the ropes. On the opposite bank they occupied well-built entrenchments, and opened a brisk fire on our approaching troops.

"Friendly natives stated that the river—swollen as it was—could not be crossed. However, I had been in the army too long to be intimidated by the opinions of so-called experts. I asked for a hundred of the strongest men to volunteer to swim the stream. The detachment easily crossed the river about a mile above the enemy trenches. I sent another company on a wide detour, by way of the Agno fords, to get behind the rifle pits.

"As soon as I received word that my men were in position, the order to attack was signaled. The flanking assault, combined with the fire from our troops along the riverbank, forced the rebels to abandon their trenches. Within two hours, using only a single axe and hatchet, the bridge was repaired sufficiently enough to allow the rest of the battalion and two field guns to cross over to the opposite shore."

By evening, Ballance's command entered Rosales—directly on the heels of the retreating enemy, but since his soldiers had not eaten since daylight, the march was halted and the men bivouacked in town for the night.

The next morning, in a raging thunderstorm, the battalions sloshed ahead on the road to Carmen. They had planned to cross the Agno River at that spot. However, the bridge had been washed away, and the water was too swift for swimming. Captain Ballance continued: "We constructed a raft made of bamboo and wooden boards. By eleven o'clock at night, all units except Company F had been transferred to the other side. The river had risen, and was so full of floating debris, that it was deemed too dangerous for the raft to attempt any more trips until morning.

"The companies that had already crossed the stream dashed on to Villasis. They arrived at the village about midnight and, thoroughly exhausted, slept in the pelting rain and mud.

"During the evening, I was informed that the Insurgents had abandoned Urdaneta. My orders were to check the city and then move on to Binalonan.

"The next day, upon reaching Urdaneta, we were welcomed by a brass band and escorted to the plaza by town officials. The arrival of the Americans was marked with great rejoicing on the part of the civilian population. Fruit, tobacco, and meat were freely distributed among the troops. And the din of ringing church bells proclaimed the news far and wide.

"After this novel and refreshing reception, we continued on to Binalonan. The march was tortuous—through deep water, thick mud, and constant rain. The scantily-clothed soldiers were suffering from colds, fever, and bleeding feet. There was some concern as to whether the men were healthy enough to fight one more battle.

"When we reached the city, we were relieved to discover that the rebels had withdrawn a few hours earlier. I was directed to occupy the town and await further orders."

General Wheaton arrived at Binalonan on November 19, 1899. The trap had been closed, but Aguinaldo, using a disguise, had slipped through the American lines. Sam Young sent a message to Manila: "Aguinaldo is now a fugitive and an outlaw—seeking security in the mountains."

General Lawton replied to Young's message: "It is my opinion that Aguinaldo should be followed every moment from now on. He should not be permitted to establish himself at any location—or again organize a government or army. Wherever he can go, an American soldier can follow—and there are many who are anxious to undertake the mission."

Late in the afternoon of November 22, Major Baldwin received an urgent note from his brigade commander: "General Lawton says that he desperately needs you and your battalion. The only orders I have are for you to rush to Tayug—and get there in a hurry!"

Leaving supply wagons behind—and under guard—Baldwin and the Third Battalion dashed to the front. Captain Kreps graphically described the forced march: "The roads beyond Cabanatuan beggered description. The continual rains had turned the trails into a sticky morass that clung to clothes and skin like plaster—and about as heavy. Whenever the sun came out for a few rare moments, the ground was transformed into a glutinous mass of dead grass and vegetation.

"Abandoned carts and carabaos were ensnared in the muddy trap. The division ambulance—with its red cross of mercy emblazoned on the side—was a discarded wreck, sunk several feet deep in the quicksand-like muck.

"Miles of bogged-down wagon trains dotted the sloppy landscape. Dirt-caked soldiers—exhibiting tireless energy—worked, cussed, and strained every muscle in their attempts to pull and push the carts across the tenacious earth.

"There never was a spectacle more illustrative of the self-reliance of the American fighting man. Each mud-splashed, swearing soldier was determined that nothing human could prevent the supplies on his wagon from reaching their destination.

"Unhampered by vehicles, we tediously slogged past the trapped carts and animals. Good-natured salutations were exchanged between our men and the struggling wagon drivers.

"On half-rations, we trudged twenty-six miles the second day. The physical strength of the troops was heavily taxed. But, with indomitable wills, they laughed and joked at the hardships. The weary battalion arrived at Tayug on November 25, and Major Baldwin reported to General Lawton for instructions."

Meanwhile, Captain Ballance's battalion had been sent back to Villasis with orders to check all roads leading from town, in an effort to learn the whereabouts of General MacArthur's column. One of Lowe's scouts intercepted a messenger who revealed that MacArthur had reached Dagupan on the 20th.

The information was relayed to brigade headquarters. Upon hearing the news, General Young sent the First Battalion to San Fabian for a much needed rest. However, the cure was worse than the disease. Captain Ballance wrote: "The three day march to San Fabian was across a deep, muddy quagmire of so-called roads. We had been informed that clothing, shoes, medicines, and fresh provisions awaited us. But when we arrived, the only articles we discovered were a few cartons of rations.

"My troops were willing and anxious to push on in pursuit of the shattered remnants of Aguinaldo's army, but further exertion was impossible. The men were sick with fever and dysentery—they were covered with lice, and their naked feet were bruised and bleeding—they had survived strictly on government rations and no rations—they had tramped through mud and water—they had swum, waded, and rafted—they had crossed fifty streams and rivers—they had been exposed to bitter cold nights without blankets or covering of any kind.

"The battalion had been the advance guard of General Young's brigade from Arayat to San Jose—fighting nearly every day. Beyond Talavera, the exhausted troops pushed on alone into Insurgent strongholds, with orders to get in the rear of the enemy army. They never failed to accomplish a single task assigned to them.

"Upon receipt of orders to remain at San Fabian, the necessity for further physical and mental effort ceased. In a single day, three hundred men collapsed from illnesses contracted during the vigorous campaign."

General Sam Young was lavish in his praise for the First Battalion of the Twenty-second Infantry Regiment: "The ability of soldiers from this battalion to fight and risk their lives throughout this campaign of privations, showed the grit and heroism of the men of this unit. Without reflecting in the least upon the many other excellent battalions of our army—I consider this battalion as the finest and most efficient that I have ever known."

Chapter Ten

THE CHASE OF AGUINALDO EAST TO BAYOMBONG

In late November 1899, intelligence reports indicated that Aguinaldo's army had been reinforced by savage, spear-carrying Igorot tribesmen. Rumors also persisted that the Insurgent leader had established his new headquarters at Bayombong—across the nine-thousand-foot mountains of central Luzon.

On November 26, Major Baldwin received orders to proceed with his battalion to San Nicolas, and then over the mountains to Bayombong. Baldwin's instructions were to prevent the dispersed rebel forces from reorganizing and to intercept small bands of Insurgents that might attempt to sneak down into southern Luzon.

Jacob Kreps narrated the incredible journey: "The march from San Nicolas to Bayombong is a six day trip for natives accustomed to mountain travel. At San Nicolas we were issued three days' reduced rations. Thereafter, the battalion was to live off the country. The natives called the road to Bayombong 'The Infernal Trail.'

"The path led over a succession of mountain ranges—so steep that ascent and descent were made over zigzag levels. At times, during the march, I was able to hear the voices of my comrades in the distance—some apparently directly under my feet, and others directly overhead. Glancing up and backwards after a steep descent, I could often see soldiers on twenty different levels—winding and zigzagging down the precipitous slope. The march was so strenuous that halts were frequently called every ten minutes to allow the men a chance to regain their wind.

"The lower mountain levels were covered with tropical vegetation, while the heights were pine-clad. In many places, along the trail, tall grass had grown over the narrow shelf. A false step meant a fatal plunge of hundreds of feet. The path led across numerous mountain streams. One day we forded the same river twenty times. Several streams were so swift that only the strongest soldiers were able to make the crossing safely. The other troops were aided by ropes and vines stretched over the water by the more powerful men.

"The battalion was dressed in lightweight summer uniforms and carried no blankets. Shoes, socks, and trousers were wet and clammy during the entire journey. The damp nights were bone-chilling, and the infantrymen slept from sheer exhaustion until the wind and cold awakened them. Then they huddled around campfires and kept warm as best they could.

"Two native guides accompanied the march, but they deserted the first night out. After the natives disappeared, we took a wrong path. Fortunately we captured an Igorot villager and pressed him into service as a guide. The Igorot was terrified when first caught, and kind treatment succeeded in only partially allaying his fear. However, he did lead the battalion over a deer trail until we finally returned to the Bayombong road. Strange to say, he was the only native tribesman seen during our passage across the mountain chain.

"At the village of Cayapa, we came upon the ruins of an old Spanish storehouse containing many bags of wet, musty rice. The rice was dried in the sun and distributed to the troops. Without this additional food, the sufferings of the battalion would have been greatly increased.

"Beyond Cayapa, the effects of the difficult march began to show on the soldiers. Many of the men were barefooted and their feet lacerated and bloody from crushed sharp stones that covered the roadbed. Others suffered from chills and fever—all had dysentery.

"Our meager medicine supply was soon exhausted. The extremely sick, and very weak, found the march unbearable. They continually watched for opportunities to sneak unnoticed into the brush. When routed out by the rear guard, the feverish, groggy soldiers begged to be left alone to die. Only by the use of threats—and sometimes actual brute force—was it possible to keep these desperately ill men up with the battalion. Several soldiers became so sick that it was necessary to carry them. Some men said that this could not be done along certain parts of the narrow path—but it was done.

"One soldier became mentally deranged from high fever. At night, his wild cries echoed mournfully across the cliffs and valleys. The constant moaning had a depressing effect upon the battalion. But, as is always the case among American soldiers, there were many men—no less sick or depressed—who were ready to meet misfortune with a joke and a smile. These troopers were always good-humored and ever ready to help a weakened comrade. They managed to maintain their composure by sheer force of will—and inspired in others the belief that nothing was impossible."

At ten o'clock, on the morning of December 2, the Third Battalion marched cautiously into Bayombong. Aguinaldo's forces were nowhere to be seen. The people of the province had been Insurgents in name only. Aguinaldo's agents had given the natives a few rifles, commissioned a couple of officers, and then fled north to their new base at Palanan in northeastern Luzon.

Captain Kreps wrote in his journal: "Our tired troops were royally received by the populace. The governor of the province proclaimed a holiday and a feast was prepared for the entire battalion.

"An American flag flew over the governor's residence. It had been specially made for the occasion by women of the community. Everywhere we went, the townspeople expressed genuine pleasure and satisfaction at our arrival. This was a strange experience for the soldiers. Towns on the other side of the mountains had welcomed us with either musket fire or sullen silence.

"Never before had we been greeted with Filipino cheers. The troops were ragged, hatless, and footsore. They suffered with fever and dysentery. Hunger had gnawed at their stomachs for six days. And now, at the end of the journey, they were treated to a banquet at which each man was allowed to eat his fill. Unfortunately, many of the soldiers were too ill to partake of the meal. The battalion was completely out of medicines, and native remedies were tried without success."

On December 8, Major Baldwin received orders to return to San Nicolas. One officer and twenty men, too sick to travel, were left behind at Bayombong. Jacob Kreps narrated the march: "The poor physical condition of the command made it impossible to return by 'The Infernal Trail.' Accordingly, the Carranglan Pass, to the south, was selected—but it proved little better. Caballo Sur, the highest mountain, taxed the strength of the men to the utmost. Heavy rains had washed the earth from the roadbed, leaving only slippery stones and boulders. Climbing the arduous path was sheer torture to the shoeless soldiers—their mutilated feet dripping a twisting, bloody trail along the craggy route.

"Near the summit of the mountain, the battalion was compelled to bivouac at an old abandoned rice storeroom. The building was infested with vermin, and there was only shelter enough for a few of the sickest men. The night wind was biting cold, and icy sleet fell in torrents. It was impossible to keep fires burning. Without blankets, the men huddled together on the frozen ground in an unsuccessful effort to keep warm. Some of the more flippant troopers used large stones as pillows—and, in a spirit that laughs at hardships, christened the place 'Camp Misery.'

"The battalion arrived at Puncan on December 11. The march had been a daily struggle for existance. The countryside was sparsely inhabited. Rice was obtained only in handfuls. The men cooked all sorts of tropical plants, but found them lacking in flavor and nourishment.

"Puncan was within a day's journey of an army supply commissary and hospital. But, we had no sooner reached the village, than we were ordered back over the mountains. A supply wagon had been sent to Puncan with rations for five days—no meat and a small amount of medicines. In grim silence, the troops turned once again to the rough and rugged heights of Caballo Sur. The dried, brown blood of the previous march marked the trail—and was replenished anew in bright red.

"Companies B and C were directed to remain at Carranglan. The rest of the battalion reached Bayombong on December 16. Two days later, Company H was sent to Quiangan—thirty-five miles distant. The rockstrewn mountain pass to this Igorot village was reported to be the only entrance to a high valley beyond. For several miles, the soldiers were compelled to scramble over fallen logs and slippery boulders. Couriers could only travel over this hazardous terrain with an escort of at least ten men. The uncivilized Igorot natives kept themselves hidden and watched every movement of the troops. Ernest Bonge, First Sergeant of Company H, was wounded by a thrown spear. Private John Kelly wandered too far from the trail and was killed—his head and arms severed from the body.

"On Christmas Day, thirty-six men of Company L—all that were able to march—were ordered to Aritao to investigate a reported band of Insurgents. But, by the time the soldiers arrived, the enemy had fled into the mountains.

"Several days later, an elderly retired Insurgent began spreading a mystical influence among the natives of Solano. In a whining, trance-like voice, he declared himself to be the 'Holy Ghost.' These were deeply religious people, and troubles immediately set in. It became almost impossible for our troops to obtain rice, and Filipino burden bearers refused to work. Even after this fraud had been exposed, his powerful presence was still felt."

Finally, after a month of trudging up and down mountains—barefooted and in freezing temperatures—the army quartermaster was cajoled into delivering shoes and warm clothing to Major Baldwin's infantrymen, but there was method to the quartermaster's madness. Once again, the Third Battalion was ordered over the mountains—and once again the Caballo Sur was scaled—only this time in a savage snowstorm.

On January 16, 1900, Baldwin's wearied command was ordered back to regimental headquarters at Arayat. Captain Kreps stated: "Throughout this difficult campaign, the battalion did not engage in any important battles. Its record was that of duty and endurance. The soldiers marched nearly five hundred miles on reduced rations, and lost more men to disease than to actual combat."

Chapter Eleven

THE CAPTURE OF AGUINALDO

During the month of January, 1900, General MacArthur redistributed his division to cover the newly extended field of operations. The American troops remained actively engaged in pursuing Aguinaldo's army and self-constituted guerrilla units.

However, the Insurgents were not the only problem confronting the Eighth Army Corps. Bands of outlaws, called ladrones, suddenly began plundering the villages. The robbers extorted money from the townspeople—and when the bandit's terms were not met, torture and murder were added to their list of crimes.

Wealthy Filipinos were at the mercy of both types of brigands. The scattered Insurgent forces also demanded contributions from the rich. In return, the rebels promised to protect the civilians from the ladrones.

Captain Kreps stated: "Native mayors and city officials were secretly approached by Aguinaldo's agents. The mayors of most towns were intimidated by death threats, and forced to collect taxes for the rebel cause. Therefore, it became essential for American forces to effectively hunt down the ladrones and all renegade Filipinos."

Additional troops continued to arrive from the United States, and General Elwell Otis soon had more than a hundred garrisons scattered throughout Luzon. Orders were issued for every important town and village to be guarded by American soldiers. Eight companies of the Twenty-second Infantry were divided among Arayat, Candaba, and San Luis. Four other units were stationed at Carranglan and Bayombong. The balance of the regiment occupied Santa Ana, Mexico, San Fernando, Cabiao, and San Antonio.

Every rumor of Insurgent forces, ladrones, or enemy weapon stockpiles was investigated. Within the protected zones, companies of American soldiers scoured the countryside day and night, while battalions and brigades operated in the mountains.

The majority of the rumors proved unfounded, but all were carefully checked out. Captain Kreps wrote: "Many weary marches, and constantly maintained vigilance on the part of our troops, soon began to have its desired effect. Isolated groups of Insurgents became disenchanted and deserted their leaders. Bands of ladrones were broken up—their weapons confiscated, and the outlaws sent to military prisons."

Search expeditions were continually sent out from garrisoned posts. Although most of the sorties were unproductive, selected regimental reports reveal the dogged tenacity with which the Twenty-second Infantry pursued the Insurgents and ladrones:

January 29, 1900

Lieutenant Admire and twenty men of Company A encountered an enemy force of approximately one hundred soldiers on the road leading to San Pedro Magalang. The rebels retired as soon as reinforcements arrived from Arayat. Six Insurgents were reported killed.

February 5, 1900

Lieutenant Admire and his detachment captured a party of ladrones, together with eight Remington rifles and two hundred rounds of ammunition. Five of the criminals were tried and sentenced to prison terms by the provost court of this command.

February 20, 1900

Company K, commanded by Captain Hannay, left camp at one o'clock in the morning and marched to Mandili, where an enemy force had been reported. They reached their objective before daylight and surrounded the village. During the subsequent action, two Filipinos were wounded attempting to escape. About a hundred suspected Insurgents were captured, along with two stolen American horses and nine Remington rifles. Forty-eight of the Filipinos were released, whereas the others were taken to Candaba for interrogation. It was later learned that these rebels were members of a battalion formerly under the command of Colonel Simon Kabigting—who was rumored as having been killed by his own men.

February 23, 1900

A detachment, under Major Frank Reynolds, was sent to Palanglang, where Insurgent General Casto Alejandrino was said to be hiding. Reynold's detail started out shortly after midnight and entered the village before dawn. The town was thoroughly searched, but no sign of the general was found. However, Lieutenant Admire discovered several enemy uniforms, and also confiscated a Colt revolver and Mauser carbine.

February 28, 1900

Lieutenant Dalton, of Company E, led a platoon of scouts to San Miguel. Lieutenant Ripley arrested a group of twenty-three Filipinos who were found in a house reloading cartridges. Two of the men were wearing Insurgent uniforms.

March 6, 1900

A detachment from San Antonio, commanded by Lieutenant Leonard, was sent in search of the Insurgent leader Garciano Garcia. At the village of Delagut, Leonard captured fifty-nine rebels, and seized three Remington rifles, six bolo knives, and a large quantity of ammunition.

March 15, 1900

While carrying messages between Cabiao and San Antonio, Sergeant Ray, of Company I, was ambushed by a band of rebels. Ray was seriously wounded but managed to escape. A platoon, under Lieutenant Ripley, was immediately dispatched to locate the sergeant's attackers. Seven suspects were brought in. Ray identified one of the Filipinos as one of his assailants.

March 23, 1900

Information was received that a group of ladrones was pillaging native villages near the mouth of the Rio Chico River. A general movement of troops was ordered to this area. A company from Cabiao searched the banks of the Rio Grande—opposite the mouth of the Rio Chico. A detachment from Arayat occupied the fords of the Chico for a distance of two miles upstream. Additional companies, commanded by Lieutenants Huguet and Leonard, scoured the countryside lying in the angle formed by the two rivers. Eight bandits were captured.

March 26, 1900

Captain Jacob Kreps assumed command of the First Battalion, Twenty-second Infantry Regiment.

April 18, 1900

Lieutenant Admire and a platoon of scouts ambushed a body of Insurgents in the Bulacan Mountains. The rebels were commanded by Benigno Aquino. Eight enemy soldiers were captured, along with several rifles and horses.

April 28, 1900

Captain H. C. Hodges and his men surprised an enemy camp near Santa Cruz. Ten Insurgents were taken prisoner. Twenty-nine rifles and nine hundred rounds of ammunition were also seized.

May 31, 1900

General Frederick Funston, commanding Company A of the Twenty-second Infantry and a troop of Fourth Cavalry, attacked a rebel concentration in the Bulacan Mountains—twenty-five miles east of San Miguel. After a fierce fight, the enemy retreated. However, heavy fire from Insurgents on the bluffs killed Captain George Godfrey and Private Perry Ethridge—both men were from Company A.

June 11, 1900

A brigade, commanded by Generals Funston and Grant, received orders to drive Aguinaldo's forces from the Bulacan Mountains. The First and Third Battalions of the Twenty-second Infantry—companies of the Thirty-fourth, Thirty-fifth, and Forty-first Regiments—and one company of Macabebe scouts attacked the Insurgent stronghold at Sibul. After several hours of battle, the enemy withdrew to the northeast.

July 16, 1900

General Funston, along with companies of the Twenty-second, Thirty-fourth, and Thirty-fifth Regiments, successfully attacked an enemy base camp at Mount Corona. Lieutenants Dalton and Leonard captured six rebels. A large quantity of ammunition was seized, and barracks were burned.

October 2, 1900

Company A, commanded by Lieutenant Wheeler, launched a night surprise attack against Filipino outposts near San Pablo and Jaen. Insurgent Colonel

Delfin Esquivel and several of his men were taken into custody. Six rifles and five hundred rounds of ammunition were confiscated.

December 9, 1900

Company I, under Lieutenant Leonard, surprised a band of rebels near the Rio Chico. The Insurgents were routed—suffering heavy losses. Eight houses, used as barracks by the enemy, were destroyed.

December 21, 1900

Lieutenant Wheeler, acting on a tip from an informant, captured Captain Estaban Quinteros. The Insurgent officer led Wheeler's men to a site where twenty-eight rebels were encamped near Jaen. The American patrol attacked the camp during the night, killing two Filipinos and seizing eight rifles and three hundred rounds of ammunition.

December 28, 1900

General Funston, with a detachment of Twenty-second Infantry scouts, surprised a group of Insurgents near Cabiao. Six enemy soldiers were killed and one wounded. One American soldier, Private William Dold, died from wounds received during the engagement.

As the year 1900 drew to a close, the unrelenting attacks by the Eighth Army Corps against rebel forces and ladrones began to cause a change of sentiment among the Filipino civilian population. Captain Kreps commented: "As soon as the natives discovered that we were able to protect them, they gave us information in return. The peaceful farmers assisted our patrols in locating and arresting hostile enemy bands. Unfortunately a few informants were tortured and murdered by the rebels. But, with the establishment of town government, and the appointment of native police under military supervision, the confidence of the people in their own safety was strengthened.

"The creation of an ever increasing number of small garrisons necessitated the distribution of military stores over an extensive area. Supplies had to be sent to many remote points—many of which were difficult to reach even during the most favorable seasons of the year. The transportation and quartermaster departments worked around the clock to get their jobs done.

"As life in Luzon began to return to normal, the duties of the army became more complicated. Natives came into headquarters, of their own accord, to take the oath of allegiance to American sovereignty. The provost court and military commission were gradually superseded by native courts, native judges, and native attorneys. But the army still exercised supervision. As conditions improved, however, it became merely 'parental watchfulness.'

"Nevertheless, there were always constant rumors of underground Insurgent groups and weapon caches hidden for future use. The ladrones were also a continual threat to peace in the villages. Despite these problems, the army worked—campaigned—administered justice—struggled with strange laws and customs—protected the Filipino adherent from the Filipino patriot—constructed roads—hauled supplies—and supervised schools."

On January 12, 1901, General Funston, Captain Kreps, and a dozen scouts were searching an area a few miles southeast of Santa Cruz. They surprised an Insurgent patrol commanded by Cecilio Segismundo. In the resulting skirmish, two of the rebels were killed, and the others fled into the city.

The mayor of Santa Cruz was a former follower of Aguinaldo, but had recently taken a loyalty oath to the United States. He still remained sympathetic to the Insurgent cause, and hid Segismundo and his men. However, the mayor convinced the rebels that further fighting was useless and suggested that they give themselves up to American authorities.

Segismundo surrendered to Lieutenant J. D. Taylor and also turned over coded dispatches from Aguinaldo requesting reinforcements. The messages were delivered to General Funston and revealed the location of the Insurgent headquarters at Palanan. Using this information, Generals MacArthur and Funston devised a dangerous scheme that they hoped would finally put an end to the fighting.

A prepared message was sent to Aguinaldo reporting that a band of guerrillas, with a few American prisoners, were on their way to Palanan. On March 23, General Funston, four other army volunteers, and about eighty Macabebe scouts—dressed in Insurgent uniforms—entered the rebel compound and captured Emilio Aguinaldo.

The revolution quickly began to fall apart. On April 28, General Alejandrino, accompanied by an orderly, surrendered to Major R. T. Yeatman, and a few days later, at San Isidro, General Lacuna and his entire command capitulated to General Funston.

Although organized resistance to American authority appeared to have ended, many Filipinos vowed to continue the war for independence. On September 28, a detachment of Ninth Infantry, stationed at Balangiga, was eating breakfast when they were attacked by a band of guerrillas. Forty-eight soldiers were killed, and their bodies mutilated.

Guerrilla activity continued to persist for a year after the capture of Aguinaldo. It was not until the Fourth of July 1902 that President Theodore Roosevelt declared the Philippine Insurrection ended.

The four years of warfare had involved 100,000 American soldiers. They fought in 2,811 separate engagements and lost 4,243 men killed and 2,818 wounded. More than 16,000 Insurgent troops died in combat, and thousands more Filipinos died of famine and disease. The monetary cost to the United States was in excess of 500 million dollars.

However, no sooner was the war declared officially over than the southern islands broke out in open revolt. American troops were sent to remote outposts on Samar, Cebu, and Mindanao. The island jungles were home to giant leeches, deadly snakes, and vicious crocodiles. Malaria, cholera, and other tropical diseases were endemic, but the deadliest menace of all was the fierce, bolo-swinging Moro tribesman.

On November 28, 1903, the Twenty-second Infantry Regiment was ordered to Mindanao.

Chapter Twelve

THE MORO REVOLT

The Moros are Moslem descendants of the Mussulman Dyaks of Borneo, and, for hundreds of years, had fought off every attempt to conquer their lands. During the sixteenth century, the Spaniards tried to subjugate the Moros of the Lake Lanao district of Mindanao, but Spanish muskets and armor were no match for the long, sharp knives of the fanatical native tribesmen.

For the next 250 years, Moro supremacy was absolute. Spain attempted to collect tribute from the islands—but the tax collectors never returned.

Early in the nineteenth century, Moro longboats constantly entered Manila Bay and raided the west coast of Luzon. Besides plunder, they carried away women and children—selling them into slavery. Several expeditions, were outfitted to put an end to the piracy—but it was not until 1860 that a fleet of steam launches succeeded in confining the tribesmen to their own islands.

In 1895, Spanish Governor General Ramon Blanco led a campaign against the Lanao Moros. Weapons and large quantities of ammunition and supplies were carried from Iligan to Marahui on the north end of the lake. Gunboats were dismantled, hauled overland in sections, and reassembled on the water. For three months, Spanish troops attacked the native cottas (rectangular earthworks, ten feet high, surrounded by ditches, and covered with thick courses of bamboo), while the gunboats bombarded every stronghold that their shells could reach.

Map 12.1
Mindanao

In a few instances, the campaign was a success. The Spaniards were able to hold the village of Marahui, but the supply route from Iligan could not be traveled without a heavily armed escort. The Lanao natives bragged that the Spanish were never able to force their way into Taraca—the Moro stronghold on the eastern shore of the lake.

Robert Hamilton graphically described the Moslem culture of these "strange" people of the southern islands: "The Moro custom of leadership is a complicated structure of religious and political feudalism. The Sultan of Jolo is the acknowledged chief. However, under him are a multitude of lesser sultans—each only as powerful as his riches and number of wives. On the second level are the dattos—likewise as important as their wealth and women. Beneath the dattos are the free Moros—and lastly, the sacopes or slaves.

"A form of government does exist, but the religious and civilian officials seem to be mere tools in the hands of the sultans. Each sultan has his own priest, lawyer and scribe.

"The greater part of the Moro district around Lake Lanao is swampy, and it is in these marshes that the tribesmen have built their cottas. Every cotta has at least one lantaca—a small brass cannon that fires slugs. The Moro warriors carry rifles—ranging from flintlocks to Mausers and Krags. Their weak gunpowder, however, gives the bullets a short range—but the nature of the country, and the character of the defenses, preclude any long range fighting. In addition to their rifle, each tribesman carries a kris [a long sword with a wavy, double-edged blade], a bolo, and one or more daggers. Wealthy tribesmen also carry spears. Every native is a veritable walking arsenal.

"The Moro is a fanatical fighting machine. If he dies in battle, he is assured a seat in heaven—and every enemy he kills will become his slave in paradise.

"Cottas can only be captured by direct assault—and in this sort of fighting, the armament of the Moro is vastly superior, and more destructive, than the American rifle and bayonet."

On December 6, 1903, the Twenty-second Infantry Regiment waded ashore on the beaches of Mindanao. The First and Third Battalions were assigned to Camp Marahui. The Second Battalion was stationed at Camp Pantar.

Captain Hamilton stated: "Upon landing, we were greeted by several sultans and dattos. They professed friendship—but in the majority of cases, that friendship was of doubtful character.

Map 12.2
Lake Lanao Region, Mindanao

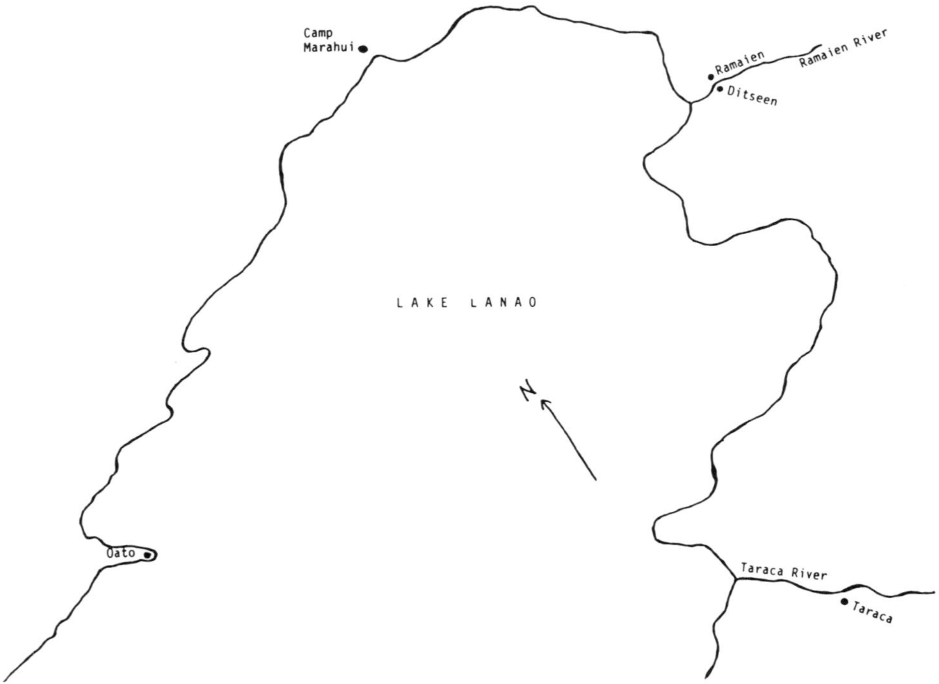

"The road between the seacoast and Marahui was declared 'sacred' by the district sultan—and no American soldiers were to be harmed along its path. In return, we were to respect and protect the Moros living in the vicinity.

"But south of Marahui—and all around the rest of the lake—there was not a spot where Americans were safe from attack. Taraca, on the eastern shore, was openly hostile. Maciu, chief sultan of Taraca, was the most feared ruler on the island. He had enlisted an army of renegades, and instilled the tribesmen with the frenzied enthusiasm and boldness of their ancestors.

"Spain's failure of conquest in the Lanao region had strengthened the Moro's belief in their own invincibility. A centuries old pride of sovereignty was not to be humbled by 'promises' of politicians—or a mere show of arms. A sultan remarked to me, 'Spaniards have come and gone. They have been followed by Americans—and, in time, why should they not go too?' "

The American presence in Mindanao was only a token occupation force, but it was like a cancerous growth to the proud Moslems. During a march around the lake, the rear guard of the Third Battalion was continually fired upon by shadowy figures—who moved silently through the jungle like ghostly apparitions.

A few days later, while duck hunting, a group of soldiers from Camp Marahui were attacked by a band of Moros near Ramaien. The commander of the Twenty-second Infantry, Colonel Henry Wygant, made repeated demands to the sultan of the district to surrender the hostile natives. However, the chieftain refused to deliver the men over to the army. After all avenues for a peaceful settlement of the issue had been exhausted, Colonel Wygant formed an expedition to arrest the stubborn potentate.

At three o'clock on the morning of January 22, 1904, the First Battalion, under Major J. S. Parke, climbed aboard several long native canoes called vintas. Their destination was seven miles across the northern end of Lake Lanao. Major Parke described the perilous mission: "Companies B and D were landed a short distance from Ramaien, with orders to advance on the village from the rear. Companies A and C, along with two rowboats carrying a Gatling gun and Vickers-Maxim gun, continued on to Ramaien.

"At the mouth of the river, leading to the village, we were met by a number of minor chiefs. The nervous chatter, and agitated behavior of the natives, plainly indicated that an attack was being meditated. With red umbrellas raised over their heads, the tribesmen dashed excitedly about—arguing among themselves until their leaders shouted for them to sit down.

"After a short parley with a couple of dattos, we paddled upstream—the gunboats leading the way. Along the route, the 'umbrella-men' screamed continuously at other Moros on the opposite bank of the river. The dattos had informed us, that although they themselves were friendly, the 'bad' Moros were the ones across the waterway.

"Ramaien consisted of several miles of cottas along the north bank of the river. Another village, Ditseen, was similarly constructed on the south shore. The river at this point was well commanded by the solid wall of cottas. Our boats would be running a narrow gauntlet. At any moment a short range, murderous fire could be opened up on us.

"I had noticed that on each side of the river—between the cotta walls and the water—a narrow trail followed the bank. Detachments of soldiers were landed and moved in single file—keeping pace with the lead boat.

"As we proceeded slowly upriver, many heavily armed Moros could be seen running from cotta to cotta. They carried rifles and knives, and evidently were hurrying to a large fortress at the upper end of town. Since this obstacle could be a menace to our boats, the land detail was directed to approach and investigate the formidable looking bastion.

"The cotta's entrance had been closed by a tall bamboo gate. Within the fort, a number of Moros could be seen with their rifles aimed at our soldiers advancing along the shore. On command, Lieutenants Campbell Flake and William Roberts, leading their men, rushed the cotta. The two officers were immediately cut down.

"The stunned soldiers attempted to deploy along the path—there was no room. They splashed into the water—and from waist high positions dueled the Moro riflemen. While the battle was going on, a few troopers braved enemy bullets and dragged the wounded officers to safety. The detachment then retreated to protective cover at the base of the bamboo walls.

"Reinforcements were rushed ashore. The angry Americans—spurred on by revenge—charged the cotta. No quarter was given or asked. The Moros quickly realized they were not dealing with the Spaniards, and attempted to flee.

"The enemy was not prepared for this kind of furious assault. There was no time to make a stand as they were chased from one cotta to another. The attack was pursued until it became evident that there was danger of our firing into the other command—which was slowly forcing its way through the swamps to the rear of the town. Cease firing was sounded, and trumpet calls kept each unit informed of the position of the other until a junction was effected.

"The battalion, assisted by the machine gun boats, drove the Moro warriors several miles from the village. The balance of troops, still aboard canoes, were put ashore and moved downriver—destroying any cottas still occupied by the enemy.

"During this engagement, our men were hampered by the proximity of supposedly friendly Moros. American flags suddenly appeared over the cottas at Ditseen. Many hostile shots were fired from the purported sympathetic side of the river. However, our trusting soldiers assumed that these bullets came from Ramaien natives who escaped across the stream. Ditseen was spared—although a large number of their tribesmen were observed carrying rifles.

"As the battalion reembarked aboard the canoes, the rear guard came under fire from a cotta that had not been completely destroyed. The Gatling gun finished the job, and the weary troops returned to Camp Marahui at five o'clock that afternoon."

Lieutenant Flake died from his wounds, and as a mark of respect, all officers were instructed to wear a badge of mourning for thirty days. Enemy losses were estimated at twenty-five killed.

Although the purpose of the expedition—the arrest of the sultan—was not accomplished, the Moro chieftain and several of his followers surrendered themselves to Colonel Wygant and made overtures for peace. However, shortly after midnight on February 27, a large Moro force attacked the Second Battalion at Pantar. Shots were fired into the campsite, and one sentinel was cut by a vicious slice from a kriss Several nights later, a similar assault was directed against Camp Marahui. It was thought that the natives were trying to get their hands on more rifles.

Because of the seriousness and uncertainty of conditions in Mindanao, Major General Leonard Wood was dispatched to the island. He arrived with the brigade consisting of battalions from the Seventeenth and Twenty-third Infantries—four troops of the Fourteenth Cavalry—and one field artillery platoon.

Chapter Thirteen

THE MINDANAO CAMPAIGN

President Theodore Roosevelt was determined that the United States establish its control over the southern islands of the Philippine archipelago. Germany and Japan were a visible threat to move in on any show of weakness. The island of Luzon, although important, would be worthless if foreign powers controlled its southern approaches.

Roosevelt had sent General Wood to Mindanao with orders to try to convince the Moros that Americans were not in the islands to exploit the natives or change their religious beliefs. However, the Moros, over the years, had learned to be skeptical of foreigners and continued to resist American presence in the islands.

Wood's strategy was to subdue the more hostile Moro tribes—and number one on his list was Sultan Maciu at Taraca. The plan was for the general's brigade to advance around the southeast corner of the lake. The Third Battalion, of the Twenty-second Regiment, would travel by boat from Camp Marahui and force a landing south of the Taraca River that could be used as a supply base for Wood's brigade.

The Twenty-second Infantry battalion embarked at two o'clock on the morning of April 2 and proceeded toward Taraca in a double column of native canoes. A heavy fog covered the lake, but the soldiers maintained contact by calling out to each other.

About 6:30, the boats were about five hundred yards from the mouth of the Taraca River. The fog was beginning to lift, and groups of excited natives could be seen running to their cottas. Moments later, the Moros opened fire and screamed threats and insults as the flotilla continued on past the river entrance.

Captain J. L. Donovan described the action: "We had native guides in each canoe. They were supposedly friendly; however, they seemed to have little knowledge of the shoreline on the eastern coast. The lake suddenly merged into a huge marsh—tall swamp grass was everywhere. Even using field glasses, we could find no solid ground suitable for a landing and supply point.

"As the boats skirted the shore, armed natives could be seen stealthily following our course. A mile south of the Taraca River, as we rounded a bend, a hundred yard break in the marsh grass revealed a small bay—and behind it, solid ground.

"Protecting the bay from the lake was a line of bamboo piles—and fifty feet inland from the shore loomed a large cotta. A band of angry Moros had congregated at the entrance. About a hundred yards from the beach, Colonel M. P. Maus stopped the lead boat. He explained to the tribesmen that we wished to land and camp there—and they would not be molested if they were friendly.

"The datto was belligerent and insolent—continually refusing to give us permission to land. The chief Moro claimed that he had women in the cotta. Colonel Maus attempted to assure the datto that no harm would come to either his women or his belongings.

"As the parley dragged on, the natives became more militant—and it was evident that reinforcements were moving in. Our boats had been disposed on the arc of a circle—broadsides toward the cotta. Suddenly swamp and cotta blazed with fire. Bullets and slugs ripped the air, striking canoes and splashing the water. Lantacas, Mausers, Remingtons, and flintlocks delivered an almost perfect volley.

"The battalion was immediately ordered to return fire. The Gatling and Vickers-Maxim guns answered without a moment's delay. A strong converging stream of bullets was poured into the cotta and beach grasses where gun-flashes had been spotted.

"Two men of Company M were wounded by the enemy's initial assault. However, our rifle and machine gun barrage disrupted the careful aim of the natives. Although boats were struck—and many slugs from lantacas splashed nearby in the water—there were no further casualties.

"After realizing that they would be driven from their stronghold, pandemonium raged within the cotta. Frenzied, demoniacal shrieks from the baffled Moslems drowned out the sounds of musketry. A few minutes later, the order was given to charge the beach. Bullets were still flying from the cotta as the canoes dashed toward shore.

"One after another, boat keels ground into the sand. Soldiers jumped into the water and raced across the beach as our machine guns covered their assault. The Moros, still screaming, abandoned the cotta and fled into the jungle.

"We quickly discovered, however, that this was only one of twenty-four forts in the vicinity. Strict orders were issued for the battalion not to advance. Enemy strongholds could be seen in all directions. We were directed to wait for further instructions. The following morning, the Second Battalion of the Twenty-second Regiment arrived—along with two troops from the Fourteenth Cavalry. They were the advance guard of General Wood's brigade.

"Throughout the day, small groups of allegedly friendly tribesmen strolled into our bivouac—some bearing white flags. Others carried American flags of Chinese make—curious thirteen-starred affairs that they claimed had been given to them by former commanding officers at Camp Marahui.

"These natives came from parts of the lake region that had proven to be hostile. But in the face of superior forces, they were loud in their assertion of friendship—especially when they saw the Stars and Stripes planted on hitherto unconquered Taraca soil."

The following day, Wood's brigade completed its march around the southeastern shore of Lake Lanao and camped on the banks of the Taraca River.

On April 5, the Second and Third Battalions of the Twenty-second Infantry attacked the village of Lalabuan and destroyed twenty-two cottas. The Moros scattered as the Americans approached, and no shots were fired.

Captain Donovan continued his account: "During the afternoon, two Filipinos—who had been slaves of one of the sultans—came in under a flag of truce.

"On April 8, we camped near the mouth of the Ramaien River. These marches were made through swamps and unbridged streams. We did not stop until late in the day, as many halts were necessary in order to investigate nearby cottas.

"The liberated slaves had told us of a cotta at Pitud. It belonged to Datto Gadapuan and was reported to contain many rifles and a large quantity of ammunition. Companies F and G, under Captain David Wheeler, were sent to investigate. Upon approaching the cotta, Wheeler's detachment came under heavy fire. For several minutes the Americans were pinned down in the swampy ground. Finally Corporal Sam Treadway exclaimed that he would rather face the datto's bullets than have snakes and leeches crawling all over his body. Captain Wheeler was of the same opinion and yelled for his men to charge the cotta. Attempting to outscream the Moros, Company F busted through the bamboo gate. It was hand-to-hand battle. A Moro swung his kris at Treadway. The corporal wrestled the knife away from the native and killed him with his own weapon. Treadway and three other soldiers were wounded in the melee—but the cotta was quickly captured.

"With the exception of Wheeler's battle, our march through the hostile countryside was unopposed. Although the mud was knee-deep, outlandishly attired delegations of flag-waving Moros continued to greet our column—pledging their allegiance to the United States. Colonel Maus was offered presents of fruits, chickens, and eggs—no strings attached—so they said. One procession was led by a native carrying a large flag taken from an American transport vessel. We thought it best not to ask him where he obtained the banner."

Captain Wheeler and his men were sent on ahead to reconnoiter upstream along the banks of the Taraca River. During the afternoon of the 10th, they came upon a large cotta. Since women and children were reported to be inside, Wheeler attempted to negotiate a surrender. The natives inside the cotta denied having guns but said they were willing to give up their other weapons.

Wheeler was dubious, and as women and children emerged from the bamboo doorway, he ordered them taken to a safe place. A few tribesmen then appeared and walked slowly out from the fort—dropping their bolos on the ground. Seconds later, fifty screaming Moros dashed from the cotta—slashing the air with their long knives. Captain Wheeler was immediately stabbed through the heart. The Americans were shocked for a moment—then a hail of bullets met the charging enemy. When the smoke cleared, there was not one Moro warrior standing—thirty were killed outright.

On April 11, the Second and Third Battalions returned to Camp Marahui. However, Companies F and G were ordered to remain at the entrance to the Taraca River. An outpost was established and named Camp Wheeler in honor of the dead captain.

The men stationed on picket duty at the outpost were in constant danger. Captain Donovan described the arduous conditions under which the soldiers lived and fought in the middle of hostile territory: "A barbed wire fence and chain of lanterns encircled the camp. Nightly attempts were made by the Moros to rush the outpost. Our bullets failed to stop the charge of these hysterical fanatics. At close quarters, their razor-sharp knives were deadly—even after the tribesmen were riddled with lead. One native—his feet shot off—crawled on his hands and knees several yards before collapsing from loss of blood. In most instances, the enemy attack could not be checked until the Moros became entangled in the barbed wire fencing.

"These unprovoked assaults were largely due to the influence of a native priest named Omar. He claimed to be a prophet with divine powers. Any native provided with charms made by Omar was said to be protected from American bullets. Three blades of grass, consecrated by the priest, and placed in the path of a sentry, would kill the guard immediately. When the charms failed to work, Omar placed the blame on the Moro who used them.

"The whereabouts of the prophet was shrouded in mystery. However, his power was increasing at an alarming rate. It became necessary to either capture him or prove the falsity of his claims.

"In early June, a rumor reported that Omar was camped in the foothills east of Delama. Accordingly, on the 15th, three companies of the Twenty-second Infantry, and a company of Philippine scouts, departed Camp Marahui by boat. They landed at Delama at daybreak and headed toward the prophet's campsite.

"Omar had boasted on numerous occasions, that if an expedition was sent to capture him, all he had to do was flash his spear and the American soldiers would drop dead.

"When the crest of the first foothill was reached, the advance guard of scouts was fired upon. A moment later, from a commanding ridge five hundred yards distant, a tall figure jumped up from the deep grass—and shrieking Mohammedan curses—shook his spear in a threatening fashion at the Americans. As soon as the scouts raised their rifles to put a quick end to the nonsense, the tribesman, assumed to be Omar, vanished. With scouts leading the way, the command raced in pursuit. About two miles from the lake, Omar's camp was discovered and destroyed. A few of his disciples were killed, but there was no sign of the priest.

"On returning to the boats, either the prophet himself or one of his men, followed our soldiers and kept up a constant sniper fire from concealed positions in the woods. If it was one of Omar's followers, he must have remained a believer in his master's talisman—since several heavy volleys into the trees failed to stop the attack from this one rifle. But, among the other Moros, the prophet's influence weakened, and the nightly assaults on Camp Wheeler were soon abandoned."

However, there were still a large number of hostile natives in the Taraca area—and it was the job of the troops at Camp Wheeler to try to pacify them. The Moros were encouraged to return to their homes and resume normal, everyday living. A few did return, but minor sultans and dattos continued to exert pressure on their subjects not to cooperate.

In an attempt to calm the people and demonstrate that they would not be mistreated, platoons were sent out on "get acquainted" marches. Captain Donovan stated: "Natives hid themselves near the camp and reported any unusual preparations going on behind the barbed wire fence. Our patrols were invariably fired upon. The cunning tribesmen set snares and traps along paths used by the companies. They were especially adept at luring officers to their death."

Daily rains soon turned the eastern lake country into one large swamp—but the troops continued to march in an effort to establish peace and order. Slowly the American influence began to take hold. Many Moros, disillusioned with their leaders, surrendered knives and rifles, and returned home to work in the rice fields.

Conditions also improved at Camp Marahui. Although the necessity of guarding the large post prevented frequent patrols, small detachments were sent out once a week into neighboring districts, but it was a continual frustrating battle for the Americans. Mindanao was like a smoldering fire. Whenever it was thought that progress toward peace was being made, the flames of war would flare up again.

On the night of July 10, Private Ben Oswald was on sentry duty at Camp Marahui. He was suddenly attacked and savagely knifed by a Moro tribesman—who also stole the soldier's rifle. The assailant was tracked to the village of Marantao, but the sultan of the district refused to surrender the culprit or the rifle.

Marantao extended for three miles along the western shore of the lake, and in the early morning darkness of August 1, the village was surrounded by companies of the Twenty-second Infantry. At daylight,

Colonel Maus gave the signal to attack. It was a vengeful assault. The Americans charged one cotta after another—completely destroying numerous forts and inflicting heavy casualties on the enemy.

Meanwhile, the soldiers at Camp Wheeler were baffled by an unusual set of circumstances. Hundreds of villagers in the Taraca district began to disappear. Native huts were found empty, and no one was working in the rice fields. Captain Donovan related: "The only logical explanation for the missing people was that they had left the lake for the mountains. But it was difficult to believe that so many natives could live permanently in the high, rocky country."

On August 12, while exploring a canyon trail, a detachment of Twenty-second Infantry suddenly confronted a large cotta that completely blocked the path. It had been built on a sharp incline going uphill. The bamboo walls of the fort were twenty feet high, and in front of the cotta was a deep ditch filled with running water. A tall, thick bamboo gate, four feet wide—the width of the trail—covered the entrance. To one side of the gate, a narrow doorway had been cut—only large enough to admit one person at a time.

Captain Donovan stated: "When our troops came within sight of the cotta, angry Moros along the high parapets shouted for the Americans to leave the area or die. The soldiers refused and the natives opened fire with rifles and lantacas.

"The infantry dashed for cover as a flood of bullets and shells sprayed the narrow trail and splattered against the canyon walls. It was quickly realized that a large force would be needed to capture the cotta, and a message was sent for reinforcements.

"In the meantime, a few scouts cautiously crept up the incline toward the gate. They had orders to try and set fire to the bamboo. However, upon approaching the rampart, they noticed that the gate opened outwards—and behind it were piles of huge boulders. Through slits in the bamboo, the scouts could see tribesmen trying to work a lever—which would open the gate, sending tons of rocks racing down the path. The scouts shot the Moros and dashed through a shower of bullets back to their own lines. The Americans rapidly retreated out of danger and waited for reinforcements."

Before daybreak the following morning, Colonel Maus and three companies from Camp Marahui arrived. Two detachments were sent up the canyon walls on either side of the fort. At the signal to charge, the Moros were caught completely off guard. While two companies rushed the bamboo gate, the others dropped into the cotta from above. Amazingly, the fort was seized without a single casualty.

Colonel Maus was very much impressed with the enemy's engineering skill: "The cotta was admirably constructed. Bombproofs had been built to protect the defenders from possible artillery fire. Beyond question, it was the strongest fortification captured in the Lake Lanao district.

"However, the size and location of this cotta was evidence of something the Moros were anxious to conceal. Upon reaching the crest of the next ridge, the mystery of the missing Taraca people was revealed. The large valley below was surrounded by a wall of cottas—and hundreds of natives could be seen cultivating the rice fields."

After the Americans discovered his new village, Sultan Maciu sent a peace delegation to Camp Wheeler to discuss the surrender of weapons.

In early September, a detachment of ninety men, under Captain O. R. Wolfe, was sent into the mountainous Cotabato district of southern Mindanao. Wolfe's orders were to capture Datto Ali—whose renegades were constantly provoking native uprisings. However, the expedition was unsuccessful, and Ali would continue to cause trouble for another year.

However, problems often arose even among supposedly friendly natives, as Robert Hamilton related: "The Sultan of Oato was numbered among the Moros professing allegiance to the United States. Accompanied by a retinue of followers and slaves, he made frequent ceremonious visits to Camp Marahui. Military authorities, therefore, were greatly surprised when his tribesmen greeted one of our boats with rifle and lantaca fire.

"This sultan's district was guarded by three stone cottas—two of them on commanding hills. The countryside was known to be rough, and in many places impassable.

"On the early morning of October 24, the Second Battalion, Twenty-second Infantry, embarked by boat from Camp Marahui and headed for Oato. At the same time, a troop of Fourteenth Cavalry traveled by land to cover the sultan's domain from the north and west. A battalion of Twenty-third Infantry and an artillery battery were sent to the south and west borders of the territory.

"The canoes, carrying the Second Battalion, reached Oato at daylight. From high cliffs overlooking the lake, the Moros promptly opened fire with rifles and lantacas. The Gatling gun boat immediately answered the attack—effectively raking the bluffs. Under protection of the machine gun, two companies were landed—and after a difficult climb up the steep hills, drove the defenders from the first line of cottas on the ridge.

"According to the original plan, the field battery was to have joined the battalion at this point—but the nature of the terrain was such that the arrival of the artillery was delayed.

"The nearest stone fort, nine hundred yards distant, had many flags flying from its ramparts. The confident Moros could be seen on the parapet—brandishing rifles, spears, and the ever dangerous kris.

"The battalion's advance was slow—underbrush, boulders, and a maze of rock walls blocked the approach to the cotta. And all the while, small groups of natives attacked our column from concealed hiding places.

"After six hours of savage combat, the first fort was charged and captured. A number of lantacas and old Spanish cannons were found. The largest cannon could fire a six-inch solid shot. Fortunately for us, the Moros did not have ammunition for this weapon.

"The troops took a short rest and then continued their advance toward the next cotta—six hundred yards away. Battle flags also flew from this fort's walls, and the ominous beat of primitive tom-toms echoed from within.

"The enemy was jubilant as they watched the soldiers move forward. The cotta was in an excellent defensive position—it could only be approached in single file. But luckily, the gun battery showed up—and just in time. The battalion was instructed to withdraw while the artillery shelled the stronghold. Thirty minutes later, the troops were ordered to storm the fort. It was captured without resistance.

"Shrapnel and shell fragments were found throughout the cotta. The walls were spotted with blood, showing where slivers of steel had found their mark. Lantacas, loaded and aimed—but never fired—indicated the hasty abandonment of the fortification."

The Sultan of Oato surrendered and declared that he would never again oppose American sovereignty. By the end of November, most of the native leaders in the Lake Lanao district had turned in their weapons and pledged their loyalty to the United States.

However, Datto Ali still remained the major obstacle to peace on the island. With consistent regularity he sent guerrilla bands out to raid villages—and even became bold enough to stage hit-and-run attacks on American camps.

In January 1905, Camp Marahui's name was changed to Camp Keithley. On March 7, Private James Morrison was on sentry duty when he was stabbed to death in a sneak attack by a band of Ali's followers. An expedition was immediately organized and landed near the mouth of the Taraca River, but the murderers were never found.

During April, a battalion of the Twenty-second Infantry was sent to the island of Jolo to put down a revolt by Moro chieftains. They arrived back at Camp Keithley near the end of June.

In late September, General Wood received information that Datto Ali could be found at his ranch on the Malola River—in the mountains of southwest Mindanao. On October 5, an assault force was organized under the command of Captain F. R. McCoy. There was no shortage of volunteers for the mission, and McCoy hand-picked a hundred men for the dangerous assignment.

In order to avoid any possibility of being spotted by Ali's spies, the detachment was sent by boat to Digas on the Davao Gulf. They landed on the 16th and were joined by ten Philippine scouts. It would be a strenuous journey over hazardous mountain trails, and any sick or footsore men were left behind—despite their protests.

With very few stops for rest, the small company of soldiers crossed the jungle-covered mountains in five days. Before daybreak, on the morning of October 22, Lieutenant Remington and the advance guard reached the datto's ranch. McCoy and the main body of troops were close behind.

Complete silence was ordered. Flank columns were sent out to surround the ranch buildings. The soldiers concealed themselves in the brush and tall grass—and waited.

At daylight, Ali and a dozen of his men came out of the main house. They were unarmed and stood on the porch talking. Remington motioned one squad forward and sent another to the rear of the building, but somebody on the porch noticed movement in the bushes. Ali dashed back in the house for his gun. At the same moment, Remington and his squad charged up the porch. The datto fired point-blank at the lieutenant. The bullet missed, but struck and killed Private Bobbs. Remington smashed through the door—his pistol blazing. Ali was hit and fell to the floor. He staggered to his feet and attempted to escape through the rear door. The second squad was waiting for him. A fusillade of bullets spun the renegade around like a top. The datto was dead before he hit the ground. The other Moros surrendered without a fight. The last organized resistance to American sovereignty in the Phillippines had ended—although isolated hot-spots of rebellion would continue for several more years.

In November, the Twenty-second Infantry Regiment received orders to return to the States, and arrived back in California on January 14, 1906—nearly six years from the date it left San Francisco.

During military operations in Cuba and the Philippines, the Twenty-second Infantry fought in more than one hundred engagements, and each company marched an average of five thousand miles.

The campaigns were hard-fought and exhausting, but they were the training ground for young officers—like Lieutenant Douglas MacArthur and others, who became the key leaders of the United States Army during the following two world wars.

AFTERWORD

This is the story of infantry soldiers told by an infantryman in the weathered pages of his knapsack diary. It is told in his terms; often you can feel his fatigue, discomfort, sacrifice, and pride. The reader of this work will feel the impact of poor planning at high levels as expressed by a soldier responsible for executing the missions in the trenches, without the proper resources. The infantryman of today can relate to the actions of the men depicted in this work. It is important that we never forget the everyday, dog-face infantryman's sacrifice and dedication to his unit and its mission required in support of his country. The warfare depicted in this book could have just as easily have been describing the infantry fight most recently in Vietnam or Panama. It is dirty, hard, and dangerous, compounded by a perpetual state of fatigue, carried out by a group of brothers working together, the infantry. The comforting thing about this work is that the feeling of bonding required for the men of the Twenty-second Regiment to accomplish the missions described in this book exists in the infantry units of today's army. The Twenty-second Infantry Regiment lives in today's army, displaying the same pride, dedication, and self-sacrifice described in this work.

James N. Joyner, Jr.
Colonel, Infantry
Virginia Military Institute

INDEX

Admire, Lieutenant, 148–50
Agno, P. I., 137
Agno River, P. I., 137
Aguadores, Cuba, 25, 27
Aguinaldo, Emilio, 53–59, 61–64, 68, 72–73, 79, 83–86, 99, 95–97, 100–109, 113, 116, 118–24, 129–31, 134, 138–43, 147, 150, 152–53
Alejandrino, General Casto (Insurgent), 149, 152
Alger, Russell (secretary of war), 69
Ali, Datto (Moro Chieftain), 170–72
Anderson, General Thomas M., 56, 59, 61–63, 66, 72, 76, 81–82, 95
Angat, P. I., 115–17
Angeles, P. I., 131
Aquino, Benigno (Insurgent leader), 150
Arayat, P. I., 120–22, 130, 132–34, 136, 139, 145, 147–49
Aritao, P. I., 145
Arizona (transport), 72
artillery regiments, U.S.: First Artillery, 125; Third Artillery, 57, 65, 72, 78, 81, 83, 85, 97, 102, 104; Fifth Artillery, 69; Sixth Artillery, 76, 81, 82, 84, 87, 92, 125, 127; Utah Artillery, 57, 62–63, 79, 81, 83–84, 98–100, 104
Astor Battery, 69, 70–71, 76
Australia (transport), 56–57

Bacoor, P. I., 128–29
Bagbag River, P. I., 116–17
Bakor, P. I., 59, 61
Balangiga, P. I., 153
Baldwin, Major J. A., 130, 133–36, 138–39, 141, 143, 145
Baliuag, P. I., 117–20, 122
Ballance, Captain John G., 14, 121–22, 132–37, 139
Bayombong, P. I., 141–44, 147
Bell, Major J. F., 85
Bigaa, P. I., 103–4
Big Horn River, 5
Binalonan, P. I., 137–38
Birkhimer, Captain, 119–20
Blanco, Spanish General Ramon, 155

178 INDEX

Bobbs, Private, 172
Bocaue, P. I., 103, 113
Bonge, Sergeant Ernest, 145
Boston, U.S.S., 85
Bruce, Lieutenant W. E., 17
Bubb, Major John, 129
Bulacan, P. I., 103
Bulacan Mountains, P. I., 113, 150
Bulango, P. I., 136
Bustos, P. I., 117–18

Caballo Sur, P. I., 143–45
Cabanatuan, P. I., 132, 135–36, 138
Cabataon, P. I., 99
Cabiao, P. I., 121, 132, 148–49, 151
Caloocan, P. I., 83–85, 97, 107
Calumpit, P. I., 113
Camp Dewey, P. I., 63, 68–70
Camp Marahui, Mindanao, 157, 159, 161, 163, 165–69
Camp Pantar, Mindanao, 157–61
Camp Wheeler, Mindanao, 166, 168–70
Camp Wikoff, 50–51
Candaba, P. I., 122–23, 130, 147–48
Capron, Captain Allyn, 30, 32, 39
Carmen, P. I., 137
Carranglan, P. I., 144, 147
Carranglan Pass, P. I., 143
Carroll (steamer), 6
Casey, Lieutenant Edward, 8–10, 14
cavalry troops, U.S.: Second Cavalry, 8, 47; Fourth Cavalry, 76, 85, 87, 89–90, 111, 113, 115, 129, 150; Seventh Cavalry, 5–6; Eighth Cavalry, 14; Ninth Cavalry, 38–39; Tenth Cavalry, 34–35, 39; Fourteenth Cavalry, 161, 165, 170

Cavite, P. I., 55, 58–59, 61, 63–64, 68
Cayapa, P. I., 142
Cebu (gunboat), 92, 153
Cebu Island, P. I., 86
Cervera, Admiral Pascual (Spanish), 24
Chadwick, Captain French, 24
Chaffee, General Adna R., 30, 39, 41
Charleston, U.S.S., 84
Cheyenne Indians, 17
Cheyenne River, 3
China (transport), 57
Cingalon, P. I., 71
City of Peking (transport), 56–57
City of Sidney (transport), 56–57
Colon (transport), 57
Concho (transport), 51
Cooke, Captain, 98, 100
Corregidor Island, P. I., 86
Cotabato, P. I., 170
Coxey's Army, 17–18
Crazy Horse (Sioux Indian Chief), 8
Custer, General George A., 6

Dagupan, P. I., 132, 139
Daiquiri, Cuba, 25–28, 46
Dalton, Lieutenant, 149–50
Dasmarinas, P. I., 130
Davao Gulf, Mindanao, 172
Delagut, P. I., 149
Delama, Mindanao, 167
Devila, General Augustin (Spanish), 56
Dewey, Admiral George, 22, 53, 55, 58–59, 61–62, 67, 84, 86, 97–98, 127–29
Digas, Mindanao, 172
Ditseen, Mindanao, 160–61
Dold, Private William, 151
Donovan, Captain, J. L., 164–65, 167–69

INDEX

Ducoureaud House, Cuba, 30, 32, 39
Dunham, Dr. Carroll, 26, 33–35, 51
Dyers, Captain, 82

Eastwick, Major, 119–20
Egbert, Colonel Harry C., 90, 98, 101
Eighth Army Corps, 58, 63, 67–68, 86, 109, 116, 119, 124, 131–32, 147, 151
El Caney, Cuba, 29–30, 32–34, 36–39, 41, 43–44
El Pozo, Cuba, 30
Esquivel, Colonel Delfin (Insurgent), 150–51
Ethridge, Private Perry, 150

Ferrer, Gabriel (mayor of Santiago, Cuba), 48
Fifth Army Corps, 21–23, 30, 41, 44–45, 49
Finley, Private, J. F., 66
Flake, Lieutenant Campbell, 160–61
Fort Abercrombie, 3
Fort Buford, 1, 3–4, 14
Fort Crook, 18, 20, 52, 75
Fort Erie, 1
Fort Felipe, Cavite, P. I., 59
Fort Garland, 10
Fort Gibson, 10
Fort Griffen, 10
Fort Keogh, 5, 7, 10, 14, 17–18
Fort Lewis, 10
Fort Lincoln, 5, 9–10
Fort Lyon, 10
Fort McKavett, 10
Fort Malate, P. I., 59, 68–70, 76, 87
Fort Rice, 4
Fort Stevenson, 3
Fort Sully, 4
Fort Totten, 3–4, 10

Fort Yates, 14
Fraine, Major, 112
French, Colonel J. W., 122–23
Frost, Colonel, 79
Funston, General Frederick, 105, 150–52

Gadapuan, Datto (Moro), 165
Gale, Captain, 113
Garcia, General Calixto (Cuban), 30
Garcia, General Garciano (Insurgent), 102, 149
Getty, Captain Robert, 37
Glendive Creek, 4, 5, 7
Godfrey, Captain George, 150
Grant, Captain F. A., 92, 111, 134
Grant, General Frederick D., 150
Grayson, Private Willie, 78
Great Porcupine River, 5
Greene, General Francis V., 57, 61–66, 68–69
Grimes, Captain George, 30, 32
Guadalupe, P. I., 83
Guadalupe Ridge, P. I., 89–90, 125, 127
Guantanamo Bay, Cuba, 23
Guerrero, Francisco (mayor of Baliuag, P. I.), 119
Guiguinto River, P. I., 104

Hale, General Irving, 78, 83–84, 87, 97–102, 104
Hall, General R. H., 97
Hamilton, Captain Robert L., 1, 3–9, 14, 157, 170
Hannay, Captain, 122, 148
Hawkins, General Hamilton, 35–36, 38
Hawthorne, Captain, 82
Helena, U.S.S., 127
Hobbs, Captain, 65–66
Hodges, Captain H. C., 150

INDEX

Hong Kong, 53, 55, 67, 92
Howard, Major, 101
Huguet, Lieutenant, 149
Humingan, P. I., 136

Iligan, Mindanao, 155, 157
Iloilo, Panay, P. I., 85
Imus, P. I., 129
infantry regiments, U.S., regular:
First Infantry, 5; Third Infantry, 97–98, 100, 113, 120, 122; Fifth Infantry, 8–9; Sixth Infantry, 5, 35–36; Eighth Infantry, 4, 5, 21, 37; Ninth Infantry, 5, 47, 125, 128, 153; Twelfth Infantry, 125, 128; Thirteenth Infantry, 125, 127; Fourteenth Infantry, 56, 59, 62, 68, 76, 81, 111, 125, 127–28; Sixteenth Infantry, 35; Seventeenth Infantry, 4, 5, 97, 161; Eighteenth Infantry, 57, 62–63, 72; Twentieth Infantry, 4, 84, 87, 92; Twenty-first Infantry, 125, 128, 129; Twenty-second Infantry, 1, 5–10, 14, 17–20, 24–25, 32, 36, 40–45, 49–50, 52, 75–76, 86–87, 89–90, 92, 95, 97–98, 100–102, 109, 112–13, 115–18, 121, 123–24, 130, 132, 139, 147, 150–51, 153, 157, 159, 163, 165, 167–70, 172–73; Twenty-third Infantry, 57, 62, 68, 72, 83–84, 161, 170; Twenty-fourth Infantry, 132; Thirty-fourth Infantry, 132, 150; Thirty-fifth Infantry, 150; Thirty-seventh Infantry, 132; Forty-first Infantry, 150
infantry regiments U.S., volunteer: First California, 56, 59, 62, 76, 82; First Colorado, 57, 62–63, 66, 69, 72, 78–79, 83, 125; First Idaho, 57, 76, 82–83, 85, 111; Twentieth Kansas, 78, 81, 85, 97, 102, 104–5; Second Massachusetts, 22, 33; Thirteenth Minnesota, 57, 70, 72, 97, 120; First Montana, 78, 81–82, 84–85, 97, 102; First Nebraska, 57, 62, 78–79, 84, 97, 99, 101–2, 104; Seventy-first New York, 22, 35–36; First North Dakota, 76, 111–13, 115–16, 121; Second Oregon, 56, 59, 62, 72, 87, 92, 97–98, 100–101, 119–21; Tenth Pennsylvania, 57, 62, 65, 78, 81, 97, 99, 102, 104; First South Dakota, 78–79, 81, 97, 99, 101, 102, 104; First Tennessee, 79, 83; First Washington, 76, 83, 87, 92–93, 106, 111; First Wyoming, 57, 76, 82–84, 97
Indiana, U.S.S., 23
Iron Star (Indian warrior), 9

Jaen, P. I., 150–51
Jaudenes, General Firmin (Spanish), 56, 67
Johnson, Private Henry W., 75, 94
Jolo, Sultan of (Moro), 157
Jolo Island, P. I., 172
Jones, Captain Frank, 93

Kabigting, Colonel Simon (Insurgent), 149
Katipunan Society, 53
Kelly, Private John, 145
Kenley, Captain, 128
Kessler, Lieutenant, 66
Kettle Hill, Cuba, 30, 34–36, 39
King, General Charles, 76, 81–83
Krayenbuhl, Captain, 65–66, 101
Kreps, Captain Jacob F., 13–17, 23, 28, 37–38, 42, 45, 49, 52, 75, 86–95, 98–99, 101, 103, 104, 107, 109, 113, 115, 118–24, 130–34, 136, 138–39

Lacuna, General (Insurgent), 152
Laguna de Bay, P. I., 58, 94–95, 109–11, 125
Laguna de Bay (gunboat), 84, 92
Lake Lanao, Mindanao, 155, 157, 159, 165, 170
Lalabuan, Mindanao, 165
La Loma Church, P. I., 79, 81, 97, 113
Lame Deer (Indian), 8–9
Las Guasimas, Cuba, 28
Las Pinas, P. I., 125, 127
Lawton, General Henry W., 21, 27, 29–30, 34, 39, 42, 95, 97, 109–13, 115–21, 123, 125, 127–29, 138–39
Lee, Captain Arthur H., 40
Leonard, Lieutenant, 149–51
Lingayen Gulf, P. I., 131–32
Little, Colonel F. C., 83
Little Big Horn River, 6
Lockwood, B. C., 36–37, 40
Long, John D. (secretary of the Navy), 55
Longos, P. I., 112
Lowe, Captain, 132–35, 139
Ludlow, General William, 21, 29, 32–33, 37, 39, 41–42, 52
Luzon, P. I., 55, 86, 94, 106, 130–31, 141, 143, 147, 151, 155, 163

Macabebe scouts (Filipino), 132, 135, 150, 152
MacArthur, General Arthur, 57, 63, 66–68, 71, 76, 78, 83–85, 87, 97–98, 100, 102–6, 113, 120, 122–23, 130–31, 139, 147, 152
MacArthur, Lieutenant Douglas, 173
McCoy, Captain Frank R., 172
McCoy, Lieutenant Colonel, 70, 79
McCulloch, dispatch boat, 53, 55, 68

Maciu, Sultan (Moro), 159, 163, 170
McKinley, President William, 20–21, 55, 64–65
Maglibutad, P. I., 132
Maine, U.S.S., 18–20
Malabon, P. I., 85–87, 98, 100
Malinta, P. I., 100–101
Malola River, Mindanao, 172
Malolos, P. I., 73, 95, 97–98, 102–7, 109, 113
Mandili, P. I., 148
Manifest Destiny, 64
Manila, P. I., 55, 58–59, 63–65, 67–69, 72–73, 76, 79, 83–84, 87, 95, 102, 110, 112, 116, 120, 125, 130–32, 138
Manila Bay, P. I., 22, 53, 59, 86, 97, 110, 125, 129, 155
Manila-Dagupan Railroad, 85, 98, 131
Marahui, Mindanao, 155, 157, 159, 161, 170
Marantao, Mindanao, 168
Marilao, P. I., 102
Marilao River, P. I., 102–3
Mariquina, P. I., 83–84
Matablan River, P. I., 136
Maus, Colonel M. P., 164, 166, 169–70
Merritt, General Wesley, 55, 57–58, 63–64, 66 68, 77
Mexico, P. I., 148
Meycauayan, P. I., 101
Miles, General Nelson A., 8–9, 22, 46
Miles, Lieutenant, 81
Miley, Lieutenant John, 48
Miller, General Marcus P., 85
Mindanao Island, 86, 153, 155, 157, 159, 161, 163, 168, 170
Missouri River, 7
Mobile (transport), 52

INDEX

Monadnock, U.S.S., 84, 127
Montauk Point, N.Y., 50, 52
Morrison, Private James, 172
Morro Castle, Cuba, 25
Moses, Lieutenant Colonel, 79, 125
Mott, Captain T. Bentley, 69
Mount Corona, P. I., 150
Murphy, Captain John, 81
Musselshell River, 5

Naguilian, P. I., 121
Nanca River, P. I., 97
Naylor, Lieutenant, 99–100
Newell, Lieutenant Isaac, 91
Newport (transport), 57, 63
New York, U.S.S., 24–25
Niblack, Lieutenant, 85
Noriel, General (Insurgent), 63
Norzagaray, P. I., 113, 115
Novaliches, P. I., 97, 99–100, 113, 116

Oato, Mindanao, 170
Oato, Sultan of (Moro), 170–71
O'Hara, Captain, 65, 81
Ohio (transport), 75
Olympia, U.S.S., 69
Omar (Moro prophet), 167–68
Orizaba (transport), 23
Oswald, Private Benjamin, 168
Otis, General Elwell S., 6–8, 58, 72, 76, 84, 86, 97, 106, 112, 116, 120, 123–24, 131, 147
Otis, General Harrison Gray, 76, 81, 85, 97–98, 102, 104
Ovenshine, General Samuel, 76, 81–82, 125, 127–28

Pacheco, General (Insurgent), 102
Padacan, P. I., 82
Paete, P. I., 112
Pagsanjan, P. I., 111–12
Pagsanjan River, P. I., 112

Palanan, P. I., 143, 152
Palanglang, P. I., 149
Panay Island, P. I., 85
Pando, General (Spanish), 29
Paranaque, P. I., 110, 123, 125, 127–28
Parke, Major J. S., 159
Parker, Lieutenant John, 35–36
Pasay, P. I., 82–83, 109
Pasig, P. I., 87, 90, 92, 111
Pasig River, P. I., 76, 78, 81–84, 90, 97, 110–11, 125
Pasunkambor River, P. I., 115
Paterno, Pedro (Insurgent leader), 116
Pateros, P. I., 92
Patterson, Colonel John H., 24, 33
Perindo, Daniel (Insurgent leader), 58
Pierce, Private Charles, 133
Pilar, General (Insurgent), 120
Pine Ridge Agency, 14
Pitud, Mindanao, 165
Plenty Horses (Brule Indian Warrior), 14
Potter, Major, 81
Powder River, 4, 6
Pratt, E. Spencer (U.S. consul general), 53, 55, 61
Puncan, P. I., 144

Quiangan, P. I., 144
Quinteros, Captain (Insurgent), 151

Rafferty, Captain M. A., 36
Ramaien, Mindanao, 159–61
Ramaien River, Mindanao, 165
Rankin, Captain W. G., 1, 3
Ray, Sergeant, 149
Reinhardt, Private William, 91
Remington, Lieutenant, 172
Reynolds, Major Frank, 149
Rio Chico River, P. I., 149, 151

Rio Grande de Pampanga River, P. I., 113, 121, 132, 134–35
Ripley, Lieutenant, 149
Roberts, Lieutenant William, 160
Rogers, Major W. P., 92
Roosevelt, Theodore, 22, 34–35, 49, 153, 163
Rosales, P. I., 136–37
Rosebud River, 6–9
Rough Riders, 22, 27, 32, 34–35, 39, 49

Samar Island, P. I., 153
Sampoloc, P. I., 78
Sampson, Admiral William T., 24–25
San Antonio, P. I., 148–49
San Fabian, P. I., 132, 136, 139
San Fernando, P. I., 121, 123–24, 130, 148
San Francisco del Monte, P. I., 99
San Ildefonso, P. I., 119
San Isidro, P. I., 113, 121, 133–34, 152
San Jose, P. I., 113, 115–16, 136, 139
San Juan, Cuba, 29–30
San Juan Bridge, P. I., 78–79
San Juan del Monte, P. I., 79
San Juan Heights, Cuba, 30, 32, 34, 38 39, 41, 49
San Juan Hill, Cuba, 35–36, 38, 41
San Juan River, P. I., 78, 99
San Luis, P. I., 123, 147
San Mateo, P. I., 113
San Miguel, P. I., 78, 113, 117–22, 149–50
San Nicolas, P. I., 132, 141, 143
San Pablo, P. I., 150
San Pedro Macati, P. I., 82–83, 87, 97, 109, 111, 123
San Pedro Magalang, P. I., 148
San Rafael, P. I., 116–17

Santa Ana, P. I., 81–82, 148
Santa Cruz, P. I., 87, 110–11, 150, 152
Santa Mesa, P. I., 78
Santa Rosa, P. I., 135
Santiago, Cuba, 23, 25, 27–29, 32, 40, 42–46, 48–49, 64
Schurz, Carl, 64
Scott, Captain E. D., 92, 127
Segismundo, Cecilo (Insurgent), 152
Segranca (transport), 24, 27
Senator (transport), 75
Seneca (transport), 51
Senn, Dr. Nicholas, 44
Seventy-third Filipino Regiment (Insurgent), 84, 123, 134
Sevilla, Cuba, 28, 43
Shafter, General William, 21, 24–29, 34, 38–39, 43, 45–50
Sheridan, General Philip H., 1
Sherman, General William T., 1
Siboney, Cuba, 26–27, 43–44, 46, 50–51
Sibul, P. I., 150
Sioux Indians, 3, 7–8, 14
Sitting Bull (Sioux Indian leader), 8
Smith, Colonel James F., 82
Solano, P. I., 145
Spring Creek, 7
Stanley, General David S., 4–5
State of Texas (transport), 49, 51
Stotsenberg, Colonel, 79, 81, 83, 101
Summers, Colonel Owen, 98, 113, 115–20
Sumner, General Samuel S., 30

Taboatin River, P. I., 135
Taguig, P. I., 92–93, 95
Talavera, P. I., 136, 139
Talinapa, P. I., 99
Tampa, Florida, 21–23

184 INDEX

Taraca, Mindanao, 157, 159, 163, 165, 168–70
Taraca River, Mindanao, 163–66, 172
Tarlac, P. I., 130, 132
Taylor, Captain Henry C., 23
Taylor, Colonel, 38–39
Taylor, Lieutenant J. D., 152
Tayug, P. I., 138–39
Terry, General Alfred H., 6
Tombo River, P. I., 134
Tondo, P. I., 87
Tongue River, 7–9
Tongue River Agency, 17
Toral, General José (Spanish), 43–44, 46–47, 64
Torres, General (Insurgent), 102
Treadway, Corporal Sam, 166
Treaty of Paris, 68, 73
Treumann, Colonel, 116
Tuliahan River, P. I., 99–101, 113

Urdaneta, P. I., 136–37
Ute Indians, 10

Van Horne, Major, 33
Villasis, P. I., 137, 139

Wassell, Captain William H., 25, 28, 32, 37, 40–41, 43, 45
Watterson, Private J. W., 69–70
Webb, Lieutenant, 79

Weisenburger, Major John J., 92, 106, 112
Wheaton, General Lloyd, 87–88, 90, 92–93, 95, 97–99, 102, 125, 127–30, 132, 136, 138
Wheeler, Captain David, 150–51, 166
Wheeler, General Joseph, 27–28, 30, 32, 46
White League, 5
White River, 14
Wikoff, Colonel Charles A., 20, 24, 41
Wildman, Rouseville (U.S. consul), 61
Wolfe, Captain Orrin R., 170
Wood, General Leonard, 161, 163, 165, 172
Wright, General Marcus, 35–36, 38–39, 44–45, 85, 100, 102–3, 105–6
Wygant, Colonel Henry, 159, 161

Yeatman, Major R. T., 152
Yellowstone River, 1, 4–7
Young, General Samuel B. M., 27, 130, 132–36, 138–39
Young, Surgeon, 84
Young, William H., 116–20

Zapote River, P. I., 128
Zealandia (transport), 57

ABOUT THE AUTHOR

A. B. FEUER is a military historian and freelance newspaper and magazine journalist. The author of *Bilibid Diary: The Secret Notebooks of Commander Thomas Hayes,* he has also published articles in numerous journals, including *Military History Magazine, Sea Classics, Civil War Quarterly,* and *World War II,* and is a book reviewer for *Military Review.*